21 Days

OF PRAYER
FOR YOUR BUSINESS

MAKING GOD
THE FOUNDATION
OF YOUR JOURNEY

BY MONIQUE MCLEAN

This book may be purchased in bulk for educational, business, fund-raising, or sales promotional use. For book orders visit shop.youinfuse.com.

© 2018 McLean Essentials, LLC
Published by McLean Essentials, LLC
Birmingham, AL

ISBN 978-0-9983457-6-5

Printed In the United States of America.
To purchase copies of this book please visit shop.youinfuse.com.

V3/1-2018

INTRODUCTION

Why hello there! I can't even begin to tell you how excited I am this little book ended up in your hands. Whether you bought it, someone gave it to you, or you found it on the side of the road, I am thrilled you took the time to peek in and see what it's all about. We are going to embark on an amazing journey together. Yep. It's about to get kicked up to crazy level up in here. You see, I know what happens when you get intentional and allow God to have control over every aspect of your life, including your business. The world thinks you have to separate the two, but let me let you in on a little secret; YOU DON'T! Before we dive into our first day's topic, let me share a bit of my story with you. After you hear my story, you will understand why I am so passionate about God being the foundation of your business.

I have loved the area of sales for as long as I can remember. It's funny how we can look back over the course of our lives and critique it, right? I think back to how much I loved candy bar sales as a kid. I couldn't wait to go out asking people to buy a bar of chocolate. I had no fear. As I grew older, I loved working in the retail environment. I was motivated, driven, and I loved a healthy sales competition. It was the one thing I felt naturally gifted at in life. It seemed easy and effortless. I enjoyed going to work each day, and I was confident in my job position. One would think I should continue down this path in life, right? Makes sense, but I'm kind of random. I decided to enroll in nursing school instead. Hey, it's a noble profession. I'm not going to argue that point. However, for the person who passed out when having her blood drawn or even walking into a hospital to visit someone, probably not a smart choice. Oh, how fun it is to look back over the choices we made in life.

In 2004 I began nursing school. Between my first and second semester, I got a wild hair and opened up an OH SO CUTE scrapbook store. Did I mention I was random? Oh boy, I like to keep life interesting. I finished up nursing school but decided never to nurse. Seriously, if you have been through nursing school, this makes no sense. Hey, it's how I roll though. I can't even begin to tell you how much I enjoyed owning this store. I felt like it was what I was made to do. I couldn't wait to go to work each day. I loved buying the product at tradeshows and interacting with vendors. Marketing and merchandising made my heart happy. Helping customers each day made me feel alive. Life was good. Our store became a huge hit, and then it "kind of" went to my head. (Sigh.) My husband and I thought whatever we touched would turn to gold. We didn't want to seek the advice of others. We thought we knew it all. That's a recipe for disaster. Take my word for it. Let me explain.

Once our store became somewhat successful, everyone began asking us to open a second location. How could this be a bad thing? This had to help us crush the competition. Wasn't that what everyone in business was out to do? I saw it as a jewel in my crown when stores closed up shop. High five, another one bites the dust. Never, did I consider the crushed dreams of others. I simply thought of myself. Many very wise people suggested sticking with one location. What did they know? They were such dream crushers. We decided to do things our own way. We paved our own path; that path became a road to destruction. In 2007 we opened a second location, by 2008 we lost it all. We lost our stores, house, car, material things, and relationships. It was the best worst year of our lives. Don't worry; I explain why in the days to follow. Long story short, we did things our own way. We were very prideful, our priorities were way out of line, and we never considered giving God control of this part of our lives. Things were about to take a drastic turn, my friend. There is something about hitting rock bottom that will do that to you.

When we were at the beginning stages of losing it all; we began attending Church of the Highlands in Birmingham, AL. It's the craziest thing. We had such a perfect peace during this horrible time. We fell in love with this church and Pastor Chris Hodges, but most importantly, we fell in love with Jesus. I would love to tell you everything was smooth sailing from there on out, but that's not the case. The next four years were our rebuilding years. Remember that nursing degree I never used? Yep, it came in handy. I began working at a local hospital in town. Jeremiah, my husband, began working at our church. Speaking of church, we were there every time the doors were open. We soaked in all we could from every message. This is where we were introduced to 21 Days of Prayer for the first time. My favorite story was how Pastor Chris launched our church with 21 days of prayer and fasting. I never grew tired of hearing his heart and vision. Jeremiah and I vowed, if we EVER did a business again, we would devote it to God. We would give Him control.

In January 2013, we had the opportunity to put actions behind our words. A business opportunity came my way, which if I were to be honest, I said I would never do. Since I had been so adamant about not pursuing this path, and because of our past failures, we decided to turn to God. (ding, ding, ding) Finally, we were doing things the right way. Our church was beginning the 21 days of focused prayer; I knew now was the time to build a strong foundation like Pastor Chris did with our church. I devoted this time to praying for a clear direction and vision. I told the Lord I wanted Him part of every aspect of this journey. I would do whatever He put before me. I would always give Him credit and point others to Him. I'm telling you; this was a GAME CHANGER. I am a huge dreamer, but the Lord blew my mind with what He did over the next 14 months.

I caught a vision during those 21 days of focused prayer time, and a foundation was built. The next thing you know, my little business was rocking and rolling. I began to hit top levels in our company in record time. Now hear me out. I worked hard. I didn't pray, then decide to sit back and watch it all unfold. I actually prayed, trusted God, and put action to my prayers. I also had an amazing team of people working with me who put in countless hours of work. I will always make sure to give credit to where credit is due. However, I will never underestimate the role God played in this whole journey. I am confident He has done way more than I could ever ask or think. I will share many examples of this in our time together over the next 21 days. Are you as excited as I am? OH. MY. WORD. I can't wait. You need to trust me. Embracing God into your business will be the best decision you have ever made.

Here are a few things you need to know before we get started. Don't let this whole prayer thing freak you out. If this is all new to you, relax. It's not going to be weird and scary. Talk to God like He is your best friend. I need you to know up front; I don't claim to be a Bible scholar. I am striving to grow closer to the Lord each day, with that being said, I still have much left to learn. We don't have to be perfect before turning to God for help. He wants us to come just as we are, imperfections and all. I want you to know I am praying for you. You have no clue how much this thrills my heart that you are devoting this time to God. Don't give up. Hang in there. I can't wait to hear the stories you will tell at the end of these 21 days.

I would like to take a second and thank a few people before we dive in. Is that okay with you? The front cover may have my name listed as the "author," but it was a team that pulled it off. Eric Hudson, Natalie Elrod, Chase Brown, and Michael Durham, I am thankful for the many hours you invested in this book. You are world changers. I hope you know you have made an eternal impact in the lives of others. To my amazing family, Jeremiah, Alyssa, and Alayna, where do I even begin? I thank the Lord we are a team. You have no clue how much I love you. It thrills me to work with you daily. Thank you to the team at IC Group. It is a pleasure to work with you on projects. You always go over and beyond to exceed our expectations. Finally, thank YOU for picking up this book and walking through these 21 days. Are you ready to do this thing? Great. LET'S GET STARTED!

TABLE OF CONTENTS

DAY One

GIVE GOD CONTROL

How high does your anxiety level go when you think of handing over control to someone other than yourself? Some personalities have a harder time with this than others. I tend to fall into the, "OH MY WORD I DON'T WANT TO HAND OVER CONTROL" category. I like to do things my way. I typically have a plan, and I want to execute it. Everyone get out of my way and let me make it happen. If you read the introduction of this book, you see how that turned out for me in my first business. Not good. I believe the first step in moving in the right direction is to hand over control to God.

YOUR PAST

Think about your past. Have you ever been like me and wanted to keep control rather than give God control? If so, take a few minutes to write out some situations that come to mind. How did those situations play out?

....

....

....

....

....

....

....

....

....

ACKNOWLEDGE HIM

The first step to giving God control is to acknowledge that we need and want Him to have control. I would like for you to think about the word "acknowledge" for a minute. How would you define acknowledge in your own words?

....

....

Let's check out the definition of the word acknowledge.

- *To say that you accept or do not deny the truth or existence of something.*

What does the Bible say will happen when we acknowledge the Lord?

> In all your ways acknowledge Him, and He shall direct your paths.
> *Proverbs 3:6 (NKJV)*

Some versions of the Bible will use the word submit instead of acknowledge. The point is to accept and do not deny Him in all of our ways. All of our ways, means ALL of our ways, even business. It's that simple.

GIVE GOD CONTROL

I hope it's okay, but I like asking questions. When you initially saw the words GIVE GOD CONTROL for today's topic, what did you think that meant? Did your mind immediately jump to things you would have to give up or do? What does giving God control mean to you? Write your thoughts out below.

....

....

....

....

....

Why is it hard to hand over control to God? What are your fears? Be honest.

....

....

....

....

By permission. From Merriam-Webster's Collegiate® Dictionary, 11th Edition ©2016 by MerriamWebster, Inc.

3

TRUST GOD WITH CONTROL

Many times people are afraid God is going to make them do something they TOTALLY don't want to do. Quite the opposite is true. He designed you specifically for a purpose, which we will dive into on day three. When you give Him control, He begins to make your path straight in the ways He uniquely designed you. Don't be fearful in giving God control. It's the safest place you can be.

SEEK AFTER GOD

I challenge you to set aside your pride today on day one. Allow God to have His proper place in your life. Tell Him you would like Him to have full control over every aspect of your life, even your business. Seek after Him with everything inside of you. Look what happens below when you do.

> You will seek me and find me when you seek me with all your heart.
>
> *Jeremiah 29:13 (NIV)*

Do you see a word used in this verse that is also used in Proverbs 3:6? I'll give you a second to read them both again. Did you find it? It's the word ALL. Acknowledge Him in ALL your ways and seek after Him with ALL your heart. He just wants your ALL. How amazing is it that He looks at our hearts? He doesn't want us to jump through ten hoops, pray two years, read fifty chapters, and perform a million "works" before we can find Him. He just says seek me with ALL your heart. You are doing that during these 21 days, and you WILL find Him. Let's pray.

> *God, we acknowledge that we need you. We need you and want you in every aspect of our lives, including our businesses. We understand that your ways are higher than our ways, and your thoughts are higher than our thoughts. We understand that you have a plan for us. You have given us a hope and a future. Lord, we acknowledge you in all of our ways, and we understand when we do that, you will make our paths straight. We are going to find you during these 21 days because we are seeking after you. Your Word says, when we seek you with our WHOLE HEART, we will find you! We love you Lord. We need you in our lives like never before. We are starting this 21 days today expecting and having faith that you will blow our minds.*

We give you full control over our businesses. We desire your guidance and direction. We have done things on our terms before, and we don't want to go that direction again. Help us stay focused these next 21 days. Keep our eyes on you. Give us wisdom and revelation daily.

Jesus, I thank you for each person who is seeking after you. Speak to people today. My words can't even compare to what one second of your presence can do in their lives. Lord may they experience you. Pour out your blessings Lord. Prepare hearts for what you have in store for them. Amen.

End today by writing out your thoughts as a prayer to God. Talk to Him like you talk to your best friend. Tell Him your hopes and fears. Tell the Lord why you desire Him to be the foundation of your business. What are you expecting from this 21 days of focused prayer?

....

....

....

....

....

....

....

....

....

....

....

....

....

....

....

....

....

....

....

....

....

....

....

....

....

....

....

....

....

WALK IT OUT

1 Reflect on a few things today. Why do you want to give God control? What does giving God control look like to you? Talk to Him about this process. Explain your fears to the Lord.

2 Commit to these 21 days of focused time with the Lord. Stick it out.

3 Start each day by telling the Lord you want Him to have control. Ask Him to open doors and guide your steps.

4 Find a friend to walk out these 21 days with you. Discuss your thoughts about each day's topic.

5 Memorize and meditate on Proverbs 3:6 and Jeremiah 29:13.

DAY 1

NOTES

NOTES

DAY *Two*

FREEDOM
FROM
THE PAST

Yay! You came back for day two. I knew you would. Let's talk about a topic that we briefly touched on yesterday, your past. I asked you to think back to times when you didn't allow God to have control over your life. Remember that question? It may have brought up some "not too fun" memories. I thought about what you might be writing down or feeling. I seriously wanted to be able to come right through the book and hug you. I wanted to sit down, look you in the eyes and tell you those moments will never define you. The truth is, we all have a past. We all have chosen to follow our ways at some point in time. Those paths usually end up pretty messy. Good news though, that is in the past.

FINDING FREEDOM

Let's begin the process of finding freedom, shall we? We can't find freedom until we know what we need to find freedom from. Today you are going to be doing some deep soul searching. It may even be a bit painful, but please, push through. Be honest and transparent in your writing. Start by thinking of your past mistakes and failures. What can you learn from them? Your failures can make you bitter, or they can make you better. They can make you sink into the depths of despair, or they can fuel you to do things differently. You can take on the role of a victim, or you can be a hero and help others find hope. We have a choice in how we view our past failures. Take a second and think about the positive things that could come from your past. How can it benefit you moving forward and helping others?

....

....

....

....

HURTS CUT DEEP

There is more to our past than mistakes and failures. Yep. While we are on the subject, let's just lay it all on the table. Raise your hand if you have ever been hurt. Have you experienced rejection? Have you felt abandoned? Anyone? Have you had words spoken over you that cut deep? Take a second to write out some of these experiences. Yes, it may be hard to do, but voicing them will be the first step to finding freedom.

··

··

··

··

··

··

··

··

··

··

I can't even begin to imagine the tears shed and the sleepless nights you have experienced. You may have dug up things you had buried very deep. You may even be questioning why this is your STORY, and rightfully so. Are you angry towards God? Can we just stop right here and let me tell you I am sorry? I am sorry you have experienced pain and disappointment. I believe when we hurt, God feels it too. This may take a while for you to accept, but I pray it doesn't allow you to stop the process of FIGHTING for freedom.

DON'T BELIEVE THE LIES

Why are we discussing such a heavy topic right here on day two? I believe it's one of the biggest obstacles on our path to success. Past mistakes, failures, and hurts not only wound our hearts, but they also get in our heads. They keep us from moving forward. They make us fearful to try again. We believe we will just repeat the same thing over and over. We will get hurt again. We will suffer rejection again. We will mess up again. Why should we even bother? We believe we are what that friend said about us. We believe we are what that spouse said about us. We believe we are what that coworker said about us. We believe we are what that boss said about us. We believe we are what that teacher said about us. Listen, we have got to find freedom over these things and understand that they keep us from living the abundant life Christ Jesus has set out for us. When you listen to these voices, they win. Do you want to get me on a soapbox? Oh boy, this fires me up. The enemy wants nothing more than to keep you from walking in the life you were designed to live. There is power in you walking out who you were made to be.

WHO ARE WE FIGHTING

I want to talk about the word "ENEMY" for a minute. What in the world am I talking about when I refer to that word? Glad you asked. Start by thinking how you would define the word "enemy." Why don't you write it out below?

....

....

....

....

See, it was a very simple word to define. Did you say it was someone who was against you, someone who hated you, or wanted to bring harm to you? Did you think about a group wanting to fight against you? All of these answers would have been correct. I know this may be tough to understand if you have just started your relationship with the Lord, but there is a constant battle between good and evil. Let me show it to you in the Bible. Please hang in there with me. I pray this isn't freaking you out. Pinky promise you will not go shred this book.

> For our struggle is not against flesh and blood, but against the rulers, against the authorities, against the powers of this dark world and against the spiritual forces of evil in the heavenly realms.
>
> *Ephesians 6:12 (NIV)*

You see, as crazy it may sound, I do believe there is an enemy that we are fighting. When we struggle with those mind games, the struggle is real. It's an actual battle. Don't make a mistake. See it for what it is. A person or situation is not actually our enemy. Our fight is not against flesh and blood. It is easy to think anyone who works against us is an enemy. However, through the scripture in Ephesians, we learn that we're not fighting people. We are fighting our true enemy, satan. The Bible says he is a thief. He is on a mission to ruin our lives. Check it out.

> The thief does not come except to steal, and to kill, and to destroy. I have come that they may have life, and that they may have it more abundantly.
>
> *John 10:10 (NKJV)*

DAY 2

SHUT. IT. UP. Did you just read that? The second part of that verse rocks my face off. Satan comes to steal, kill, and destroy. Jesus comes to give us life. Not just life, but abundant life. That fires me up! I am ready to throat punch the enemy, aren't you? We have been given weapons to demolish him. OH, IT'S GAME ON!

> For though we live in the world, we do not wage war as the world does. The weapons we fight with are not the weapons of the world. On the contrary, they have divine power to demolish strongholds. We demolish arguments and every pretension that sets itself up against the knowledge of God, and we take captive every thought to make it obedient to Christ.
>
> *2 Corinthians 10:3-5 (NIV)*

What do you think is one of the best weapons we can use against the enemy? If you said the Bible, you get fifteen million gold stars. Ephesians 6:17 tells us to use the sword of the Spirit, which is the Word of God, to fight these battles. The Bible is filled with truths to replace the lies the enemy tells us. I encourage you to dive into the Bible and begin to demolish all of those fears, failures and lies from your past that keep you from living the abundant life set before you.

EXAMINING YOUR PAST

I would love for you to write out a few more thoughts. What are ways your past mistakes, failures, and hurts have jeopardized or could jeopardize your success in business?

....

....

....

....

....

....

....

....

....

Thanks for being honest and real. I know for me, I allowed my past failures and hurts to paralyze me for four years. I was a huge dreamer, but after everything crashed and burned, it made dreaming a little scary. I also allowed hurts from friendships to keep me from developing connections with others. I love to dream, and I love people. Isn't it interesting those are the two things the enemy went after? I remember the day I found freedom from these failures and hurts. I know I wouldn't be where I am today had I not found that freedom.

I believe giving God full control is the first step in the right direction on this journey you are on with your business. Walking in freedom is hands down the next best thing you can do. Please understand this is a process. We could fill this whole book on the subject of freedom, but we must close out today. Let's pray.

Jesus, you know our hurts, fears, failures, and pains. Today many people were open and honest, digging up some things they may have buried very deep. I pray you give them the peace only you can give. My words can't even begin to bring what you can bring to the table. Wrap your loving arms around them and may they rest in you. They may not physically see you, but how I pray they can feel your presence so strongly, wherever they are. I pray they will begin to see freedom over past hurts and failures. Open their eyes to how living captive to those failures, thoughts, and hurts are keeping them from being who you made them to be. You want us to live in freedom. Thank you that we can find that through you. Freedom is why we need you on this journey and why we give you control. We can't do it on our own terms. We need you leading us, guiding us, and reminding us who you made us to be. When we do it on our own terms, we feel worn down and defeated. When we allow you to have control, we begin to walk in freedom. Thank you for your freedom. Thank you Jesus, for the freedom my friends are finding in you. Help them take captive every thought and make it obedient to what your Word says. I can't wait to see what is in store for them. I love you Jesus. Amen.

WALK IT OUT

1. Ask the Lord to show you areas from your past you have buried deep that are negatively impacting your life. How is this paralyzing you from moving forward?

2. Write a letter to those who have hurt you. Tell them how you feel. Don't send that letter. Ask God to help you forgive that person and let go of the offense.

3. Forgiving and letting go doesn't mean feelings and emotions won't come back to the surface. When they do, turn to God rather than embracing those emotions. Don't fuel those feelings by discussing with others.

4. Let's kick it up to crazy level. Read Ephesians 6:13-17. These verses explain the importance of putting on the whole armor of God. Commit the verses to memory.

5. Freedom is a process. Memorize and meditate on Ephesians 6:12-17, John 10:10, and 2 Corinthians 10:3-5.

NOTES

....

....

....

....

....

....

....

....

NOTES

DAY *Three*

YOU ARE
UNIQUELY
MADE

hope you are ready for a pretty exciting day! I know yesterday was a bit grueling, but that's in the past. We are walking in freedom from our past. See what I did there? Oh, I crack myself up. Today we are going to have loads of fun. Yep. We are going to discover your unique design. I am giddy. I hope you are too.

YOU ARE CRAZY SPECIAL

Many verses in the Bible talk about your unique design. You do realize you are special, right? You are so very special. Let's look at some verses that will make this point very clear. David had it all figured out in the passage below. He was confident in his design. I pray that after today you can say the same thing. Let's check out what David said.

> For you created my inmost being; you knit me together in my mother's womb. I praise you because I am fearfully and wonderfully made; your works are wonderful, I know that full well. My frame was not hidden from you when I was made in the secret place, when I was woven together in the depths of the earth. Your eyes saw my unformed body; all the days ordained for me were written in your book before one of them came to be.

Psalm 139:13-16 (NIV)

Do you believe that about yourself? You were knit together. You are fearfully and wonderfully made. I believe this with everything inside of me. There is no mistake in your design. Look at this verse that speaks of you as "handiwork."

> For we are God's handiwork, created in Christ Jesus to do good works, which God prepared in advance for us to do.

Ephesians 2:10 (NIV)

If you think for one second that you were an accident, you better think again. You are handiwork, prepared for a particular purpose. That just screams special. There is a plan for you. Don't take my word for it, check this out.

> For I know the plans I have for you, declares the LORD, plans to prosper you and not to harm you, plans to give you hope and a future.

Jeremiah 29:11 (NIV)

YOUR GIFTS

How are you uniquely made? Can we discuss that for a bit? I want you to think of all the ways you are gifted and talented. What are those things you are crazy good at? What comes naturally to you? What are your strengths? Many people find this hard to write out. You are probably thinking how easy it would be to write out the exact opposite of what I'm asking, right? Oh, we can give someone a list a mile long of all the things we are not good at. We can talk about our weaknesses all day long. Maybe it's because we don't want to seem prideful. Maybe it's just human nature to see our flaws over our beauty. Things are about to change my friend. Even if you have to sit here all day long, I expect you to write out the beautiful gifts you possess. I can be a tad bit bossy. I'm going to see it as a gift and not a flaw. I kid. I kid. Actually, I'm not...get to writing. Please.

DAY 3

....

....

....

....

....

Those AMAZING qualities you listed out above are ways you are uniquely designed. They are your gifts. Let's see what Paul says in the Bible about our gifts.

> We have different gifts, according to the grace given to each of us. If your gift is prophesying, then prophesy in accordance with your faith; if it is serving, then serve; if it is teaching, then teach; if it is to encourage, then give encouragement; if it is giving, then give generously; if it is to lead, do it diligently; if it is to show mercy, do it cheerfully.

Romans 12:6-8 (NIV)

This verse makes me laugh. I hear Paul saying, HELLLLOOOO, here are your gifts...okay, use them. I mean he could have just listed the gifts, but instead, he went a step further to show how to use them. If it's teaching, teach. If it's serving, serve. I could totally be off in my reading between the lines, but I mean hey, it sounds like what he's doing to me.

Let's look at this a different way. Imagine it's your birthday and I am giving you a gift, actually two gifts. I have them both wrapped up nicely and you are so excited to open them. Once you tear into the packaging, you discover you have been given a fishing pole and a football. Excellent gifts, I know. Don't be disappointed, just work with me here for a minute. You have a choice now to do something with these gifts. You can put them up on a shelf somewhere and never use them, or you can use them. Pretty simple. If you've been given a fishing pole, fish. If you've been given a football, play football. You know you have received a gift before and that sucker just went right to the closet and was never seen again. The same applies to the gifts God has given us. We can use them, or we can put them on the shelf.

COMPARISON STEALS YOUR JOY

Have you ever experienced gift envy or gift comparison? Maybe you have attended a party and someone received a gift, that in your mind, is way better than the gift you received. I believe many times we get caught up in the same scenario of thinking with the gifts God has given us. If we could just be more gifted in sales like Madison, if we could just be bubbly and fun like Kari, if we could just be more of a hostess like Stacy, if we could just understand the product like April. We are so caught up in what others have; we forget to see what beautiful qualities we possess. Don't let comparison steal your joy. You are unique and special in your own way. The gifts you have been given are not only for the benefit of you but the benefit of others. If your gifts go unused, or you are so distracted by what others are and you aren't, then other people miss out on your exclusive design. Don't shelve your gifts.

YOUR UNIQUE DESIGN

I would like to end our time together before we pray by having you write a bit more about your unique design. Not only do you have specific gifts and talents, but you are also designed with a unique personality. I believe the qualities of your personality are comprised of gifts and strengths. These are just a few characteristics you may possess. Are you driven, a leader, a visionary, a problem solver, a people person, the life of the party, friendly, a hostess, loyal, a good listener, motherly or fatherly, level-headed, organized, a strategy developer, a planner, detail focused? The list could go on and on and on. Think about some of your strengths and write them out. How can you embrace these in your business? Don't focus on how other people have found success with their unique design; focus on your design.

DAY 3

DAY 3

....

....

....

....

....

....

....

....

....

....

....

....

Once you begin walking in the ways you are uniquely made, you start to SPARKLE and SHINE. You stand out. People are drawn to what you do. Look what all has been accomplished in these three short days. You have taken a huge step by giving God control. You are beginning to find freedom from your past. You are now seeing the ways you are uniquely made. I can't wait to see what the remaining days hold for you. Let's end the day in prayer.

Jesus, thank you for the ways you have uniquely crafted and designed us. I know you have created each and everyone reading this for a specific purpose and mission. There is not one mistake in the way you formed my friends reading this today. They are not an accident. I know you have created them for such a time as this, this moment we are living in today. Jesus, help us recognize the times we compare our gifts to others. We understand comparison steals our joy. We thank you for knitting us together with specific gifts, talents, and strengths. We are grateful for all you have given us. We don't want to put our gifts on a shelf. Show us ways we can use them in our businesses. We use our gifts in worship to you! Help us point people back to you as we are using the gifts you have given us. Thank you for every little detail of our personalities. We are fearfully and wonderfully made. Lord, my friends who are having a hard time seeing their unique design, reveal your handiwork in their lives. We love you, Jesus! Amen.

WALK IT OUT

1 This may make you uncomfortable, but I trust you will find the guts to do it. Ask a friend or family member to point out your gifts and talents. What do they see to be your strengths in life?

2 Encourage someone today by pointing out the gifts and talents they possess. I am positive this will make their day.

3 Study your personality. I personally prefer the DISC profile. Understanding how you and those you work with are wired will be VERY beneficial to your business.

4 Memorize and meditate on Psalm 139:13-16, Ephesians 2:10, Jeremiah 29:11 and Romans 12:6-8.

DAY 3

NOTES

....
....
....
....
....
....
....
....
....
....
....
....
....
....

NOTES

DAY 3

NOTES

DAY *Four*

CATCHING
A VISION

Hello again! Day Four. I'm not sure which day has been my favorite so far. Day One, GIVE GOD CONTROL. Love it. Maybe it was FREEDOM FROM THE PAST on Day Two. Oh, that's a must. YOU ARE UNIQUELY MADE on Day Three. That fires me up! Today we are talking about VISION. I seriously don't think I can handle all the excitement. I pray the Lord totally opens your eyes today to a vision for you and your business. Are you ready?

VISION IS VITAL

Let's just jump right in with a question. How do you feel when you have no vision or direction? What emotions are you experiencing?

....

....

....

....

Here's what the Bible says regarding a lack of vision. Let's look at a few different versions of Proverbs 29:18.

Where there is no vision, the people perish... *(KJV)*

Where there is no revelation, people cast off restraint... *(NIV)*

When people do not accept divine guidance, they run wild. *(NLT)*

No matter which translation you read, you understand that vision, revelation, and divine guidance are needed. What happens when we don't have these things? We perish, we cast off restraint, and we run wild. Did your feelings match up with these descriptions? Clearly, we need vision. We don't want to be running aimlessly through life. Vision is not just for a select few; everyone is meant to have it. So how do you find it? Great question! Let's read the following verse.

Thy Word is a lamp unto my feet, and a light unto my path.
Psalm 119:105 (KJV)

WHAT IS VISION

When you get down to the meaning of vision, it is the ability to see, correct? Vision is seeing what is right in front of you. It's reading the words on this page. You are seeing these words. Vision can also be defined as the ability to see a direction or path for our life. When we don't have this, we feel like we are in the dark. To see in the dark, you need what? Light. Let's read Psalm 119:105 one more time and take note where this light is found.

Thy Word is a lamp and light. How amazing! Turning to God and His Word will bring the light we need for vision. You may need to read this section a few times and let it sink into your mind and heart. So many times we are trying to turn the light on ourselves. We create light, manufacture light, read about light, and search for light. The whole time the answer is right there in front of us. It's His Word. The Bible is our guide and our map to navigate this journey.

ONE STEP AT A TIME

Before we move on, I would like to share a story that came to my mind when I read this verse. When my girls were little, we had the bright idea to take them on a "lantern tour" of a massive cave in Tennessee. Needless to say, it was VERY dark. They handed us each a lantern and off we went exploring the cave. The lanterns emitted only enough light to see the steps right in front of us. Our mission was to get to a huge waterfall that was deep in the cave. We couldn't see our destination, but we could see one step at a time from the light we were holding in our hand. The longer we walked one step at a time, the closer we were getting to the waterfall. Eventually, we could hear the roar of the water; we even felt the mist it was putting off. We finally arrived. We couldn't physically see the end destination when we set out on our journey, even though we knew it existed. We simply had to hold our lamp and allow it to be a light to our feet and path. I believe the same is true on our journey of life. We have to take it one step at a time and allow God to light our way.

I would love to tell you exploring that cave by lantern was a trip my girls loved and will go down in history as the best trip ever. Oh boy, that wasn't the case. When my youngest daughter Alayna and I got to the waterfall, we realized we were missing two family members. We could not find my husband and my oldest daughter, Alyssa. We walked around forever in the dark, holding the lantern up to people's faces to see if it was our missing crew. We finally found them sitting on a bench. Alyssa was in the midst of a major panic attack, and Jeremiah was

DAY 4

praying with her. Did I mention it was VERY DARK? As I write this, I have a mix of emotions. I want to bust out laughing, and then I feel horrible all at the same time. Listen, this journey can be scary, lonely, and dark. Thankfully we have a Heavenly Father we can go to just like Alyssa went to her earthly father. He will do more than light our way; He will comfort us and give us strength to keep on keeping on.

The brave people who set out on the expedition that night in Tennessee had a choice. They could forge ahead on their own with no light, or they could take one step at a time allowing the light to direct their path. This light gave them vision. Allowing God to be your light, is vision. Forging ahead with no light is doing things our own way. It leaves us wandering around aimlessly through life with no direction. Think about how dangerous this would have been in that cave. It's the same in life. Remember, without vision, we perish. Which path would you want to take? Let's pray.

Lord, we love you. Thank you so much for being a lamp to our feet and light to our paths. I thank you for each person reading about vision today. Open their eyes to what you have set before them. I pray for those who feel as if they have no direction. Help them trust in you and seek after you to guide their steps. We thank you that you order our steps. We are grateful to you that you make our paths straight. We don't want to walk around aimlessly. We want you to guide us. Lord, we trust you on this journey. We believe you will open the doors that are to be opened, and close the doors that need to be closed. We want your perfect plan, not our plan, but your plan. Make our vision crystal clear. Jesus, we hide your Word in our hearts. Bring your Word to our minds as we walk along this journey. When we face certain obstacles, bring verses to our minds to help us overcome them. We seek after you to be our guide. We need you. We love you. We thank you for everything you have done and are going to do. Thank you Jesus, for everyone who is devoting these 21 days to you. Bless their lives, speak to their hearts, and draw close to them as they draw near to you. Amen.

DAY 4

WALK IT OUT

1 Find a quiet place to sit and spend time in worship. Turn on some worship music and be still. Rest in His presence.

2 Ask the Lord to work in you these 21 days. Ask for a GOD VISION, one that is birthed by Him. You are giving Him control. You are moving in the right direction.

3 Have faith that God will lead you in the best direction. Ask the Lord to open and close doors. Pray for wisdom and discernment.

4 Memorize and meditate on Proverbs 29:18 and Psalm 119:105.

DAY 4

NOTES

....

....

....

....

....

....

....

....

....

....

....

....

....

NOTES

DAY *Five*
BE
INTENTIONAL

I am so thrilled you keep coming back for another day of focused prayer for your business. So far we have given God control, started walking in freedom from our past, seen the ways we are uniquely made, and looked at vision in a whole new light. Today I would like us to focus on the importance of being INTENTIONAL. You see, we can read things and understand concepts, but we need to be intentional with applying those things to our life and business. I want so badly for you to understand the topics we discuss daily, however, my prayer is you take what you read and APPLY it to your life. That is where real life change begins to happen. It is where understanding meets intentionality. It is where momentum and motion start to take place.

WHY ARE WE NOT INTENTIONAL

Have you ever read a book or attended a workshop and walked away thinking how simple the topic was that they covered? You could have written that book or taught that class yourself. I recently heard an amazing message at church on the theme of stress. While the message was inspiring, I found myself with a horrible dilemma. I knew all the things he was saying, however I wasn't walking them out. We understand the importance of being intentional, so why do we have a hard time embracing it in our daily agenda? Why is it difficult to put action behind the things we know will be good for our lives? Share a few of your thoughts.

DAY 5

I'm not sure what keeps you from being intentional, but for me, it typically boils down to lack of focus and being too busy. Do you ever feel like you are juggling ten million balls in the air? We live in a world that is pulling for our attention in so many ways. The loudest or the closest thing to us at the time is what usually wins our attention. I found this true while trying to finish up this book. Right now I am sitting in a house on the beach typing up day five. Yesterday I had finally had enough. I tried for weeks to focus at home. Every little need that popped up seemed more important. Oh, I had the vision. I had every chapter mapped out. I even had the cover completely designed and ready to go to print. Intentional writing time was all that was left to finish this project. I looked at my husband

and told him I had to get out of the house to focus. I sent a message to the team of people I work with and told them I would be MIA for the next 19 days. We threw clothes in the car, all my exercise stuff (that's a whole other book), stopped at a grocery store to load up on food, and then hunkered down to write. Now let's just see if I can stay focused while at the beach. If you are reading this, I must have finally got it accomplished. YAY!

Enough talk about me, let's talk about you. Do you mind if I ask a few more personal questions? I'm just getting all up in your business. I can be a tad nosey.

What does a "day in the life" look like for you? How does your typical week go down? I know this may sound silly, but I would love for you to write out all the little details of how you spend your time. Day to day, week to week, and month to month. Take some time and examine every aspect of your day.

....

....

....

....

....

....

....

....

....

....

....

....

DAY 5

WHAT DO I VALUE

I hope that wasn't too exhausting. Seeing all the things listed out in one place that pulls for your attention can be very overwhelming. It also can be very eye opening. I want you to examine the list above and write out what is most important to you. What MUST get into your daily agenda? What is a non-negotiable in your life? If you think of things that are important to you that did not make it on the list, write them out as well.

....
....
....
....
....

The things you listed out above are what you value. There isn't a master list that's right or wrong. It's simply what's valuable to you. You begin to feel off balance when your values fail to make it into your daily life. Many times we believe we have to do it all to feel balanced, that's just not the case. Saying yes to every single thing that comes your way can leave you stressed out, especially if it pushes your values out of the way. What are some time wasters that fill up your day? What do you say yes to that doesn't line up with your values?

....
....
....
....
....
....

If you struggle to be intentional with your time, I challenge you to memorize and think about these verses. They have been game changers for me.

Teach us to number our days, that we may gain a heart of wisdom.

Psalm 90:12 (NIV)

Stand at the crossroads and look; ask for the ancient paths, ask where the good way is, and walk in it, and you will find rest for your souls.

Jeremiah 6:16 (NIV)

We need to number our days and make them count. We need to ask where the good way is and walk in it. We need to be intentional. When we figure this out and walk in it, we will gain a heart of wisdom and find rest for our souls.

DAY 5

BEING INTENTIONAL WITH OUR VALUES

I hope you didn't put your writing pen away. I have a few more questions for you to close out the day. One of the biggest light bulb moments came for me when I realized the importance of embracing my values in my business. If my values are important to me, then why would I not want those in my business? My top five are God, family, wellness, growth, and bringing others hope. It doesn't matter how much success I find, when these don't make it into my business, I can feel it.

Start by narrowing your values down to your top five. Remember, these are what you hold of high importance.

....

....

....

....

....

Think about your values and how you are intentional with them. How are your values currently showing up in your business?

....

....

....

....

....

What can you start doing to embrace your values more in your business?

....

....

....

....

DAY 5

Are you doing anything in your business that goes against your values? How can you make changes to line up your actions with your values?

....
....
....
....
....
....
....
....
....
....

Thanks for being open, honest, and intentional. Let's end in prayer and I'll see you back here tomorrow.

Jesus, we love you so very much. We thank you for designing us with unique passions and values. Lord, we need your help. Teach us to number our days. Life can get so busy. Many things pull for our time and our attention. We stand at the crossroads and ask for the good way. We will find rest for our souls. Jesus, we will gain a heart of wisdom. We realize our lives are but a mist. We will make each day and each moment count. We know you have us here for such a time as this, and we will be intentional with what you have put before us. We ask for wisdom in how we spend our time. Help us to discern what to say yes to and what to turn down politely. We will be laser-focused on the mission you have set out for us. Open our eyes to the distractions that are put before us. I thank you for those who are devoting this time to you. I thank you that they are being intentional and giving you a place in their lives and businesses. I pray their values become crystal clear and you show them ways they can embrace those values in every aspect of their lives. Continue to make yourself known to my friends reading this book. I pray they experience your presence each and every day. We love you Jesus. Amen.

DAY 5

WALK IT OUT

1 Write out your top five values on several note cards and place them where you can see them often. Be intentional with these values and fight to get them in your day.

2 Commit to taking at least one time waster and eliminating it from your daily agenda. I believe in you. You can do it!

3 High five for sticking with this focused time of prayer for your business. You are being intentional. YAY you! Keep on keeping on.

4 One of my favorite series from Church Of The Highlands is called "Five." This was a game changer for me. Set aside time to check it out. You can watch at http://youinfuse.com/videos/five.

5 Memorize and meditate on Psalm 90:12, Jeremiah 6:16, and James 4:14.

NOTES

....
....
....
....
....
....
....
....
....
....
....

DAY 5

NOTES

DAY 5

DAY *Six*
ALWAYS
GROWING

re you ready to start another day of focused time with the Lord? I am so excited you are sticking this out and being intentional with giving God top priority in your life. Remember, when we seek after Him with all of our heart, we will find Him. You have acknowledged that you need Him in control of every aspect of your life; that's the greatest thing ever. I am confident He is directing your steps and will continue to make your paths straight. I am thankful you are finding rest for your soul as you ask where the good way is and walking in it. I pray today you sense His presence in your life in a very real way. Now let's get started.

EMBRACING GROWTH

Yesterday we talked all about being intentional. One of the best ways we can be intentional in our life is to always be growing. Why do we have a hard time embracing growth? Does pride get in the way? Growth means we may not have it all together. If I admit I need to grow, does that mean I look weak and foolish? Am I saying I'm not equipped? Am I admitting I don't measure up? We should always look at growth as becoming stronger, not validating our weaknesses. Pride is sneaky and can keep us from the abundant life Christ has for us. Look at what the Bible has to say about pride.

> Pride goes before destruction, and haughtiness before a fall.
>
> *Proverbs 16:18 (NLT)*

PRIDE PREVENTS GROWTH

When we allow pride to creep in and deceive us, it destroys our lives. What did we say the enemy was out to do in day two of our time together? The enemy is out to kill, steal, and destroy. That screams destruction to me. What better way to keep us from becoming stronger, than to fool us with pride? Pride says you have it all figured out, you have it going on, and you are a genius when it comes to business. Everyone needs to stop and take note of all your amazing qualities. You have nothing left to learn. Pride also comes in and tells you others are going to look down on you if you admit you need to grow. What will people think if they see you don't have it all figured out? Have you ever had any of these thoughts? If you buy into these lies and don't embrace growth, you stay in your current state. We are going to take these thoughts captive, replace lies with truths, and begin growing. Who's with me?

Before we move on, take a few minutes to write out ways you have allowed pride to keep you from growing over the course of your life. Ask the Lord to bring moments to your mind and share them below.

....

....

....

....

....

I appreciate you taking the time to think deeply about each day's topic. My prayer is these topics bring encouragement, not condemnation. I pray they open your eyes to things you may not have seen. My biggest times of growth have come from answering questions such as these. So thank you for investing in yourself and being intentional with this study. I am confident you are going to see the fruit from your labor.

GROWTH REQUIRES STRETCHING

Pride isn't the only thing that keeps us from embracing growth. Can you think of any other reasons we steer clear of this process in our lives? We pray for growth, then the second we are walking through a difficult situation that is sure to grow us, we are praying for an escape route. No? Just me? I hate to be a Debbie Downer, but growing requires stretching. Stretching can be very painful. It's way more comfortable to stay the way we are. I recently started going to the gym and my trainer said he wanted to stretch my iliotibial band. I have never felt pain like that before in my life. I was confident he was trying to kill me. I couldn't believe he was causing me this discomfort, and I was allowing it. While stretching that band was painful, it was needed for me to experience growth. There are many exercises I struggle with because of that tight band. Over time, as I embrace the pain of stretching, those activities will become easier for me to accomplish. No pain, no gain. Got to love that saying, right?

As I am writing this book, I am currently walking through a stretching season in my life. Thankfully our business continues to grow and expand, which means "I" have to grow in the process. I'm at a point where it's not physically possible to have my hand in every aspect of our business. For someone who naturally likes to take charge and be in control, this is a ton of stretching. Painful stretching.

DAY 6

I have to cast a vision and communicate it well to my team. That part isn't too hard. The hard part comes in letting go of control. It's not that I don't trust my team, I do. They are amazing! I just really like control. Maybe I need to go back and read day one of this study! Hang in there with me. I'm a work in progress.

So what is it for you? Are there areas in your life that you need to stretch? Has your comfort led to complacency?

....
....
....
....
....
....
....
....

GROWING THROUGH TRIALS

Have you ever looked at your trials as an opportunity for growth? There is a verse in the Bible that encourages us to consider trials pure joy. Let's read it together.

> Consider it pure joy, my brothers and sisters, whenever you face trials of many kinds, because you know that the testing of your faith produces perseverance. Let perseverance finish its work so that you may be mature and complete, not lacking anything.

James 1:2-4 (NIV)

Yep, you read it right. The hard times we face in life, if embraced, can grow us. As much as we want to throw in the towel and stop the painful process, it is producing perseverance through faith. Once that is finished, we are mature and complete. I believe this is yet another reason we don't like to embrace growth. Growth is a process. We like to snap our fingers and be complete. We live in a time where we want things instantly.

DAY 6

If you look in the Bible, you see story after story of people who walked in a wilderness period or dark time and their faith grew. Joseph, thrown into a pit, sold into slavery, that doesn't sound fun. Moses wandered 40 years in the desert. sweet, sign me up. How many disciples ended up in prison or beaten? Sounds like a trial to me. Jonah's journey was a piece of cake. Do you remember the story of the fiery furnace? The lion's den couldn't have been that bad. How about confronting a giant with a rock and a slingshot? We could sit here all day and list story after story, but I think you get the point. What trials have you faced in life? Have you walked through dark times? When were you at your lowest? As difficult as this may be, would you please spend a few minutes writing some of those hard times out below?

....
....
....
....
....
....

Thank you so much for reliving what may have been some of your darkest moments. I can't imagine what some of you may have experienced. Walking through a hard time is never easy. It can be dark, scary and lonely. While I may not know what you have walked through, Jesus does. He is a friend that sticks closer than a brother. He gives peace in the most difficult times. My prayer is you find peace through your pain. This peace can only be found in Jesus. I'm confident these times will produce perseverance. You will become mature, complete, and lacking nothing. Before we move on, are you able to look at your trials and see ways they have produced growth in your life? If so, list some of those out below.

....
....
....
....
....
....

DAY 6

Whew! Take a breath. I feel like we all need a group hug. That was some heavy stuff. Now let's move along.

GROWTH AS A VALUE

Let's end today by discussing specific ways we can grow. Growth is a huge value of mine. Even though it can be painful, I try hard to embrace it. I enjoy reading books and attending workshops. I love to sit, think, and analyze things I've gone through. I try finding ways to grow my strengths. I ask questions and lots of them. I find people I look up to and ask for a few minutes of their time. I soak up their wisdom. However, I am coming to discover that running to God and His Word is where I am experiencing the deepest growth. I believe now is the perfect time to close out in prayer and ask for His wisdom. Let's pray.

Jesus, we love you so very much. We thank you for all the many ways you are stretching us and growing us during these 21 days. I ask that you open our eyes to the all the ways pride and complacency can creep in and keep us from a path of growth. We know we haven't arrived. We acknowledge that we are a work in progress and we want to embrace growth on this journey. We take captive the thoughts that keep us from growing. We replace lies with your truths. Jesus, help us as we push through growing pains. We want to have perseverance, build our faith in the process. Show us areas in our lives that need growth. Give us wisdom and discernment as we walk out this path. Lord, I pray for any of my friends that are walking through a dark time, a season that is a wilderness. Bring them peace in their pain. May they feel your loving arms wrapped around them. Lord renew their strength, may they run and not grow weary. Jesus may they experience your perfect peace through stormy seasons. I pray they sense your presence like never before. Again, I thank you for all you are doing in the lives of those who are drawing close to you during these 21 days. Continue to bring wisdom and revelation as we seek after you. Amen.

DAY 6

WALK IT OUT

1   I am confident you are experiencing growth during these 21 days. Embrace the stretch and the process. It will be worth it, I promise.

2   Spend time journaling as you walk through different seasons. When you read these in the future, you will be amazed at how much you have grown.

3   Think about specific topics we have discussed that hit home in your life. Find additional verses in the Bible that specifically deal with that area and commit them to memory.

4   Memorize and meditate on Proverbs 16:18 and James 1:2-4.

NOTES

NOTES

DAY *Seven*
DON'T GIVE UP

Why hello there! Can you believe we are finishing up our very first week of the *21 Days of Prayer For Your Business*? We have covered a lot the last few days, now haven't we? Are you hanging in there? Good, don't give up. Speaking of giving up, that's our topic for today. Did you know when you hand things over to God, begin walking in freedom, understand your unique design, catch a vision, become intentional, and embrace growth, you can still feel the pressures of giving up? Oh, you can, trust me. I need you to listen to what I'm about to say, are you ready? If you quit, you will never know what could have been right around the corner for you. Quitting was almost my story on February 15th, 2013. Let's take a trip down memory lane. I pray my story encourages you never to give up.

MY FAITH TESTED

Back in January 2013, I decided to devote 21 days of prayer to a possible business venture that was running through my mind. I told the story at the beginning of this book. If you didn't read it, hurry, flip back and get caught up. I'll wait on you. Now, back to the story. I walked away from those 21 days confident I had a vision that was straight from God. I knew for certain I was on the right path. I felt my sparkle come back. It had been forever since I felt that feeling. I was back in the saddle. Game on, ready to go after it, then February 15th happened. Yep, I remember it like it was yesterday. It was about 20 days after my completion of the 21 days of prayer. I was at a crossroads, and I had to make a decision. Let's set the stage of the events leading up to February 15th.

Money was tight for our family as we started 2013. I had quit my nursing job back in August of 2012 and had no plans of returning to that career. I had sold everything I could find in our house to keep us afloat. Jeremiah was working full time at our church and picking up extra hours on nights and weekends at my dad's business. I was having yard sale after yard sale. Jeremiah was fixing phone screens in his spare time. Even with all the extra work, money was STILL tight. Do you know the feeling, the pressure of living paycheck to paycheck? Have you experienced the paycheck running out before the next paycheck arrives? Yep. This was the story of our lives.

Our youngest daughter's birthday is in January. We had to postpone her birthday party that year to February 1st when Jeremiah got paid. We knew going into the month of February we would have just enough money to get to month end. I had received my very first paycheck from the new business venture I prayed about; it was a whopping $54. Epic, I know. Small as it was, I still knew I was on the path the Lord had set out for me. As we drove to Alayna's birthday party, which consisted of one cookie cake and everyone drinking water, we had a slight problem arise. Our car broke down. Seriously? The very first day of February was starting out AWESOME. It was about to get even better. When it rains, it pours.

A couple of days later, guess what happened? Our car broke down yet again. At this point, my positive attitude was starting to slip quickly away. What in the world? Why couldn't we catch a break? I mean hello, I prayed for 21 days. I had my sparkle back. I had given God control. What was going on? I finally pulled myself together and found a few more phone screens for Jeremiah to fix. I sold a few more things around the house and then it got even worse (insert dramatic music). We got a phone call from Jeremiah's sister. Surprise, she was getting married in two weeks, and we had to find a way to get to Louisiana. Wait. Hold up. I didn't mean her wedding was a bad thing; I meant the timing couldn't have been worse. Our car was broke, we were broke, and driving requires gas money. What were we going to do? We didn't even have clothes appropriate for a wedding. Panic set in. That's the day my story almost took a different path. Let me take you there and replay those defining moments.

It was early in the morning. My girls were still in bed asleep. Jeremiah was getting ready for work while I sat in bed working on my computer. My little business was starting to pick up a bit, and I loved what I was doing. I felt alive again. Before Jeremiah left for work, we decided to discuss our current money situation. He told me the place that fixed our car said we could pay them over the next few months. His mother was sending us a check to cover our gas to get to Louisiana. We still were going to come up short though, especially since he wouldn't be able to pick up extra work while we were in Louisiana. We finished up the conversation and he leaned over to kiss me goodbye. I will never forget the feeling I felt as he walked out our bedroom door.

Heaviness washed all over me. I can feel it even as I share this story with you. It brings tears to my eyes. I felt like I was doing such a disservice to my family. I had the capabilities of driving right up to a doctor's office or hospital, put in an application, and our money worries would be over in a flash. The problem was, I knew I wasn't meant to go down that path. I sat in my bed and cried and cried. I was mourning a dream I had only embraced for less than a month. I was mourning a vision. I was mourning my sparkle. I felt so selfish. I felt guilty. I felt hopeless. Finally, I had enough sense to message some friends and ask them to pray for me.

I am confident the Lord knew what He was doing when He placed Kelli Wright, Anna Wight, and Natalie Elrod in my life. He was aware that I needed them when I was at my lowest. With tears streaming down my face and a heavy heart, I sent a message to my friends explaining my dilemma. They already knew the hard times we were facing. They also knew the sparkle I embraced back into my life. They knew the time I devoted to prayer for this new journey. They knew how badly I didn't want to go back to nursing. I poured out my heart to them in a message and hit send. It was only a matter of minutes before the encouragement began to pour in. They prayed for me. They spoke life over me. They told me not to give up. I am telling you, instantly the heaviness washed away and was replaced with peace. I had faith that everything was going to work out and be okay. Do you know how the Bible defines faith? Let's check it out.

> Now faith is the substance of things hoped for, the evidence of things not seen.
>
> *Hebrews 11:1 (KJV)*

Even though I couldn't see what was around the corner, I had faith the Lord was going to work it out. I often wonder what my life would look like right now had I made a different decision on February 15th. I would have still had my family. I would have still had God. We would probably have a decent life. I wonder if I would have lost my sparkle? Would I be thriving? Would I be walking in my unique design? Would I be writing this book? Would I be encouraging others to never give up? Would I be showing others how to embrace God into every aspect of their lives, even their businesses? THAT is what fulfills me. THAT is what I was mourning that day on February 15th, my possible future.

Let me tell you something. You have sought after God. You have found freedom from your past. You have discovered your gifts and talents. You have caught a vision. You have decided to be intentional. You are embracing growth. The enemy is freaking out. Why? When a person hands things over to God, finds freedom, knows their gifts, catches a vision, decides to be intentional, and embraces growth, it is a powerful thing. You have kicked it up to crazy world changer status, and there is nothing the enemy wants more than to keep you from moving forward. He comes to kill, steal, and destroy. He wants to kill your dreams. He wants to steal your peace. He wants to destroy your destiny. In Jesus name, that is not going to happen. We are more than conquerors. The weapons we fight with are not of this world. The weapons we fight with demolish strongholds. The enemy will not steal our hope and future. We WILL walk in the abundant life Christ Jesus has set out for us. Man, I am fired up. I hope you are too! Let's close out the day in prayer.

Jesus, we love you so very much. We want nothing more than to walk in your presence daily. We seek after you. We draw near to you. Lord, I am confident you have a hope and a future for all of my friends reading this today. I may not know their story, but you are aware of their story. I pray you give them God dreams. Dreams birthed from you. I pray you give them vision. I pray that they know, that they know, that they know when they hear from you. Give them a perfect peace when they are walking in the path you set out for them. When the enemy comes to kill their dreams, steal their peace, and destroy their destiny, help them stand strong. Giving up will not be in their vocabulary. Giving up is not the plan you have set out for them. They will not fall prey to giving up. I pray you place friends in their life that will encourage them to keep on keeping on. When times get hard, remind them to run to you. When they feel like throwing in the towel, bring verses from your Word to their hearts and minds. I thank you for what you are doing in each and every life. I thank you for what you are going to continue to do. We will run this race to completion. I know you are raising up world changers and I thank you for what you are going to do in and through their lives. Be with my friends today Jesus as they go about their day. I pray they experience your perfect peace wherever they are at on this journey of life. We love you Jesus. Amen

I have a little assignment for you before we part ways. Think about why you are so passionate about the path you are pursuing. Why are you devoting this time to prayer for your business? Do you have a God vision? Do you have dreams? What is it that is pulling at your heartstrings? I would like you to write a letter to yourself encouraging you never to give up. You heard me right. Don't laugh. There may be a point in your life that is your February 15th. A time when you are at a crossroads and have to decide if you throw in the towel or if you keep pushing forward. Talk yourself off the ledge. Remind yourself why you are walking this path. I pray if that time ever comes in your life, this letter will encourage you to keep on keeping on. Now get to writing, please.

WALK IT OUT

1 Take a picture of the letter you wrote today and save it on your phone. You never know when you might need to read over it.

2 If you are currently walking through a hard time, find someone to talk to. Don't forget to take your worries and concerns to the Lord.

3 Find someone you know is struggling and tell them to NEVER GIVE UP.

4 Memorize and meditate on Hebrews 11:1 and Romans 8:37.

NOTES

DAY 7

NOTES

NOTES

DAY *Eight*
LIVING A LIFE OF WORSHIP

Week two is about to begin. Are you as excited as I am? I wish I could sit and chat with each of you and hear your stories. I get so giddy thinking about you devoting this time to the Lord. I seriously want to jump up and down and clap my hands and scream WOOOOHOOO! Why? Because I know when we walk in HIS ways, they are the BEST ways. You, my friend, are on the right path. Whatever you imagine the Lord can do, prepare to have your mind blown. It's about to get crazy good up in here! Let's check out what His Word says.

> For my thoughts are not your thoughts, neither are your ways my ways, declares the Lord. As the heavens are higher than the earth, so are my ways higher than your ways and my thoughts than your thoughts.

Isaiah 55:8-9 (NIV)

Now let's read verse 8 in a different translation. I love it!

> My thoughts are nothing like your thoughts, says the Lord. And my ways are far beyond anything you could imagine.

Isaiah 55:8 (NLT)

THAT is the reason I am giddy. You are giving God control. You are seeking after His ways, and His ways are far beyond anything you could imagine. How exciting! You are moving in the right direction. Speaking of moving, let's get on with today's topic, LIVING A LIFE OF WORSHIP. How would you define worship in your own words?

....
....
....

WORSHIP IS MORE THAN MUSIC

I grew up in church my whole life. For many years I thought of worship as the time of singing and praying before the pastor brought the sermon. I mean only makes sense, right? You have a "worship" pastor or "worship" leader that leads you in "worship" music. I was entirely correct in my thinking. This was worship. That time of singing and prayer was a time of honoring God. We were declaring our deep love for Him, His goodness, His faithfulness, and our need for Him. We were praising Him and worshiping Him. However, this isn't the only way we can worship God. We can worship Him with our lives. Let me explain.

WORSHIP WITH YOUR GIFT

Have you ever heard so clearly from God that it was almost an audible voice? I know that may sound crazy, but it has happened to me on a few occasions. One of those times was directly related to the path I am on now. It was during the 21 days of prayer in 2013 that I devoted to this new possible business journey. I was sitting in my tiny spare bedroom listening to worship music. A song came on by Darlene Zschech, and she just has this way of bringing you into the presence of God. I sat there and was just soaking it all in. That's when I started this little conversation with the Lord.

Me: Lord, I wish I could sing like that.
God: I didn't give you that gift.
Me: Ummm, wow, okay.
God: What you sense is that she is using the gift I gave her in worship to me. It just happens to be singing.
Me: OH.
God: You can do the same thing with the gifts I gave you.

You guys, listen up. This moment right here changed my life. That conversation above might not be profound to you, but it rocked my world. This is why I pray you hear from God during these 21 days. When friends have asked how they can pray for me while I write this book, I tell them to simply pray you hear from God. I can write a bunch of words and slap them in a book, and you can read them. Fantastic. I want more than that for you. I want you to have an encounter with the living God. One second with Him can do more than ten books I write, and you read. It wasn't Darlene's singing that changed my life that day. It was the presence of God that she ushered in by using her gift in worship to Him.

My vision became crystal clear that day. I had no clue what my end picture would look like on this new business venture, and honestly, I still don't. One thing I did know, I was going to use my gifts and talents in worship to my God. I told Him that day I would do whatever He put before me. I wasn't quite clear on how I could worship Him with my gifts in a "business" environment, but I was up for the challenge. Worship is honoring. I want to honor Him with ALL that He has given me, starting with my unique design. I told Him that day I would always shout His name and point others to Him. If He opened a door, I would walk through it. I asked Him to please never leave me. I needed His help with whatever He put before me. Can I tell you something? He has blown my mind. His ways have been far more than I could have ever imagined. I would love for you to think again about your unique design. List your gifts and talents out and ask the Lord to show you ways you can use those in worship to Him.

....

....

....

....

....

....

....

....

....

....

WORSHIP IN EVERYTHING

So, here's the deal. Let's not stop with our gifts and talents. I'm all about kicking it up to crazy level. Go big or go home. How can we worship Him with other things He has given us? What about our time, money, relationships, and conversations? We actually can live out a life of worship. We can honor God in every aspect of our lives. When Jeremiah and I began to see our giving of tithe as worship rather than obligation, oh man, it changed our lives. Seriously. It was during that 21 days of prayer in 2013 where we had a heart change. It was no longer we have to do it; it was now we get to do it. Lord, we give this money back in worship to you. We thank you for being our supplier. It's your money. We look at being generous with our money as worship to God. If we leave a nice tip at a restaurant, we are doing that in worship to God. We ask the Lord to use our house in worship to Him. We do. Lord, let our house be a place where others can come, and we can show them you. Jesus, I honor you with my time. Lord, may my conversations be worship to you. I want to honor you with my words and in my relationships. Hey, if we are going to worship, let's dive all the way in baby!

Can you think of ways you can worship the Lord with your time, money, relationships, and conversations?

....

....

....

....

....

....

....

....

....

....

....

Why should we live a life of worship? Why should we honor Him with our unique design, time, money, relationships, and conversations? Write out your answer then we will close in prayer.

....

....

....

....

....

....

....

....

....

....

....

Jesus, we love you so very much. We worship you and honor you. We praise you and thank you for all the wonderful things you have done. You have restored our souls. You have brought us hope. You make a way for us when there seems to be no other way. You lead us and guide us. You comfort us. You are our defender. You are our protector. You are our supplier. Your mercies are new every morning. You are faithful. Every good and perfect gift comes from you. You are our Father. You are our Savior. You are our friend. You are our healer. You are all of these things and more. You look past our faults, our sins, the times we turn from you, and you love us anyway. How can we not worship you? You paid the ultimate sacrifice for us, your life, so we do the same. We give our lives back in worship to you. We offer you our gifts and talents. We offer you our time and our money. We give you our relationships and conversations. Each and everything that we do, may it be in worship to you. I thank you, Jesus, for my friends participating in this 21 days. I pray they experience you in their lives in a mighty way. Amen.

WALK IT OUT

1   **Think of all the ways you are blessed. Maybe even write those blessings out in the note section provided for today. Thank the Lord for those blessings.**

2   **Ask the Lord to show you ways you can use those blessings to bless others.**

3   **Commit your gifts and talents to the Lord. Ask Him to use those in worship to HIM. Thank Him for your unique design. You are such a world changer!**

4   **Memorize and meditate on Isaiah 55:8-9.**

NOTES

NOTES

DAY *Nine*
EMBRACING EXCELLENCE

Why hello there! Are you ready for day nine? Today's topic is one I have to pray about very often in my life. Understanding the difference between living with excellence and being weighed down by perfectionism. This topic consumes my thoughts and steals my peace more than I would like to admit. I have to take captive thoughts and replace them with the truths of God's Word. We will focus on living a life of excellence today. Tomorrow we will tackle perfectionism head on. Does that sound like the "perfect" plan to you? Good. Let's get started.

EXCELLENCE OR PERFECTIONISM

When you saw the word "excellence" in today's topic, did it immediately make you feel a little queasy? Let's start right here at the beginning and set the record straight. There is a difference between embracing excellence and being a slave to perfectionism. Excellence is obtainable. Being perfect will never happen. Excellence will uplift you. Perfectionism will make you feel defeated. You were not made to be perfect. You were made to live a life of excellence. Let me explain what I believe this looks like. Hang in there with me.

When you embrace excellence in your life and business, you are embracing your unique design with the tools and resources you currently have on hand. Now, hear me out. Jesus is perfect. We are not perfect. We constantly have to fight our sinful flesh; that's the reason we need Jesus in our lives. Rest assured, today's post is meant to uplift you, not make you feel defeated. One more time, we are not talking about being perfect. Let's move on.

So how do you embrace excellence in your business? Glad you asked. The first thing you need to understand is that you can't say yes to every single thing that comes your way. You have to say no to many "good" things so you can embrace a few things with "excellence." For some people, this is the worst form of torture on the face of the planet. We can't embrace excellence if we are spinning our wheels trying to do it all. That is perfectionism, probably with a little dose of pride. Don't strive for perfectionism. You weren't made to do it all.

GOOD OR BEST

Remember earlier when we talked about being intentional with our values? You listed out things that were important to you and things that were time wasters. We have to say no to time wasters, but we also have to say no to things that may be good. Good is not always the best. We can spin a million plates and be average, or we can pick a few and spin them with excellence. Let's begin by making sure we embrace our values with excellence in all we do. If you don't mind, list out your values again below. What things do you want to make sure you embrace with excellence in your life and your business?

....

....

....

....

....

....

....

I mentioned this earlier, but I want to say it again. When you embrace excellence in your life and business, you are embracing your unique design with the tools and resources you currently have on hand. Take note of the word "currently." Your tools and resources may change over the course of your journey. The way you walk out excellence may look different depending on what resources are available to you at any given time. In October of 2014, I took a group of leaders in my business to Walt Disney World for some fun and business training. I would not have been able to do that in October of 2013. Does that mean I wasn't embracing excellence in my business in 2013? No, it means my financial resources looked different in 2014 than 2013.

One of my only resources the first few months of 2013, besides prayer, was TIME. We were not in a place financially that allowed me to invest a ton of money on business tools and resources. I had to walk out excellence with my TIME. I often heard from friends that the time I was investing was not worth the money I was making. Logically, I would have had to agree with them. However, I saw my time as an investment at that stage of my journey. Time was a resource I currently had on hand. I had to make the most of it. Look back to your list of time wasters from day 5 (page 34). When we allow those to consume our lives, we are choosing average over excellence. Please read those words in the most life giving way possible. We will never be perfect, but let's try to make the most of what we have been given. Knowing is half the battle. The more we can recognize what they are, the quicker we can begin walking in excellence.

Before we move on from the subject of time, let's make sure one thing is clear. Just like your resources may look different from season to season on your journey, the same is to be said for your time. It's easy to look at a physical resource like money and give yourself grace. If the resources aren't there, the resources aren't there. Simple. Time, on the other hand, we look at through a different lens. No matter what season you are walking through, 24 hours will always be in a day. Right? Wrong. Well, actually you are right about the amount of hours, but how you need to spend them may look different. Let me give you a couple of examples. What about a new mom who just brought home her first bundle of joy? What about a person caring for a sick family member? The amount of time they both have to give to a work project may look different than it did in a different season of their life. Excellence is making the most with time you currently have on hand. If you are walking through a season that gives you less time to work with, give yourself grace. Do what you can and enjoy the season. You are in that season for a reason. Embrace it. Can you think of seasons in your life where your resource of time varied from one to the next? Share those times below.

....

....

....

....

....

....

....

GROW YOUR STRENGTHS

Let's discuss another way you can embrace excellence in your business. We mentioned it last week. Grow your strengths. Sharpen your gifts and talents. Work on the things you are naturally good at and love. So many times people think they need to spend all their time working on their weaknesses. Of course, this isn't a bad thing. However, enhancing what you are already naturally good at screams excellence. Team up with others and staff your weaknesses. When you spend all your time in areas of your weaknesses, you get little accomplished. The life is sucked out of you. If you dislike spreadsheets, find someone who loves spreadsheets. If you aren't good with numbers, find someone who is good with numbers. Together you will walk out excellence. If you don't know anyone you can team up with, pray the Lord sends someone your way. I am sure you have a talent that will benefit them as well. Maybe they are praying for someone that is uniquely designed just like you. What are areas of your business you honestly just don't enjoy? What skills do you feel like aren't the wisest use of your time? List them out below. Ask the Lord to staff your weaknesses.

....

....

....

Finally, be a student of excellence. What do I mean by that? Study people and companies that you believe do things with excellence. For me, I do this with our church, Church of the Highlands in Birmingham, AL. I study how our church does things all of the time. They are intentional with everything they do. I look at their strategies. I look at how they handle their finances. I watch how Pastor Chris speaks. I pick it all to pieces. Find people who are one step ahead of you and ask them a ton of questions. Can you think of a few individuals or companies from which you could learn? Do they embrace your same values? What stands out about them? Share your thoughts below.

....

....

....

....

....

Well, that wraps up today. It wasn't as bad as you thought it was going to be, now was it? I pray you see excellence is obtainable and is very different from perfection. We are going to kick perfectionism to the curb tomorrow. Be prepared. GAME ON. Why don't we close out the day in prayer, then following the prayer I'm going to leave you a verse to think on throughout the day. Let's pray.

Jesus, we love you. I thank you so much for all you are doing in the lives of those participating in this 21 days of focused prayer for their businesses. Lord, pour out divine revelation and wisdom each day. Reveal things we have never seen before. May we experience you. Jesus, today we are talking about "excellence." Lord, we know we aren't perfect, but we want to be intentional with all you have given us. We want to be intentional with the gifts, talents, and resources we currently have on hand. Jesus, show us ways we can embrace excellence with what you have given us. Give us the discernment to know what paths to walk on, what roads to turn down, and what opportunities to say yes to in life. We don't want to waste a second of the time you have given us. We want to be intentional. Show us ways to grow in our strengths. Show us ways to staff our weaknesses. Most importantly, we realize and acknowledge that we need you in all we do. This journey is about you. It's about eternity. The path we are all on is an avenue, a road to point others to you. When we walk in your ways, we know THAT is embracing excellence. We love you Jesus and thank you for using us and for working through us. Amen.

Think on this today. When we remain in Him, we will produce fruit. I am pretty positive His fruit is excellent.

I am the vine; you are the branches. If you remain in me and I in you, you will bear much fruit; apart from me you can do nothing.

John 15:5 (NIV)

WALK IT OUT

1. **Commit to growing in the area of your gifts and talents. Focus on growing stronger in the things you are naturally gifted at in life.**

2. **What are you passionate about? What lights a fire inside of you? Incorporate that into your business. Spend time adding fuel to that passion.**

3. **Find a mentor who aligns with your values and allow them to speak into your life. This may be someone you meet with in person or someone who inspires you from afar.**

4. **Memorize and meditate on John 15:5.**

NOTES

NOTES

DAY *Ten*

PERFECTIONISM WEIGHS YOU DOWN

Can you believe it? We are almost half way through these 21 days of prayer. Don't give up. Keep sticking with it. Continue to draw near to God and seek after Him. I am praying you see breakthroughs in your life and business. I pray you do more than just exist. I pray you thrive. Do you know one way we can start to thrive? We can kick perfectionism to the curb. Yep. Yesterday we talked about excellence. Don't confuse excellence with perfectionism. There is a drastic difference. Let's see it for what it really is and begin to weed it out of our lives. You ready? GAME ON!

PERFECTIONISM

Here are a few things a perfectionist may deal with over the course of their journey. See if you can relate to any of these characteristics. A perfectionist is rarely content. They finally get a project perfect; then they see all the ways it could have been "just a little bit" better. A perfectionist sets unrealistic expectations for themselves and others. They are so caught up in the end project being perfect; they don't enjoy the process. A perfectionist will let failures get in their head and slow them down. They never start something because they are too busy trying to make it perfect before they begin. A perfectionist feels like they have never done enough, given enough, or loved enough. The feeling of guilt consumes them often. Stressed out, overwhelmed, and worn down define their lives most of the time. When a plan doesn't come together, they snap. Comparison torments a perfectionist. Their weaknesses stand out to them like a neon flashing sign. They are critical of themselves and others. Should I keep going? I know this person far too well. For years I have let perfectionism have control over my life. I am finding freedom. I can't say that I am "perfect" at keeping perfectionism from rearing its ugly head in my day, but that's a good thing, right? That means I am giving myself grace and enjoying the process of growth in this area. Perfect will never happen, and I am okay with that. Do you deal with perfectionism? If so, write out the feelings that consume your life because you carry the heavy weight of perfect.

....

....

....

....

....

....

Check out what the Bible says about perfectionism. It is so true.

> Farmers who wait for perfect weather never plant. If they watch every cloud, they never harvest.

Ecclesiastes 11:4 (NLT)

How do you work at overcoming perfectionism in your life? Great question. First, understand our topic from yesterday. When you embrace excellence in your life and business, you are embracing your unique design with the tools and resources you currently have on hand. We have to start by giving ourselves grace. We can only do what we can do. We can't compare our season to another person's season. I was in full on sprint season from 2013 to 2015, and it came to a crashing halt. I was exhausted. I needed a period of rest. That is very hard for a perfectionist. Why? Because they think sprinting is the perfect way. They see other people in a season of sprinting and feel so guilty because they aren't doing enough, loving enough, or being enough. Before you know it, the guilt switches to the season of sprinting. Did they neglect important relationships? Are they horrible for working so hard? Should they have maintained a marathon pace instead of a sprinter's pace? OH. MY. WORD. Are you exhausted yet from all that perfectionism? I sure am. Can you think of times that you have compared your season to another person's season? If so, explain below.

....

....

....

....

....

....

....

....

....

NOT THE HOSTESS WITH THE MOSTEST

We talked about this on day three, but knowing how you are uniquely made is critical in fighting perfectionism. When you know who you are, you know who you aren't. For instance, I do NOT care for cooking. I'll do it, but it's just not my thing. I'm also not "little miss hostess." We have people stay at our house often. There was a day when I would exhaust myself trying to come up with a nice breakfast for when people woke up, snacks throughout the day, and an excellent evening meal. That didn't last long. Now I make sure to stock the fridge and pantry with items that are easy for people to grab and eat. I tell them the ground rules when they arrive. Hello, my name is Monique. I am not the best at being a hostess. Therefore, there is food in the fridge and pantry. Make yourself at home. If it's here in the house, you can eat it. If you want to cook something, there is the drawer with the pots and pans. I am not kidding. I say this every single time. I realize I just made a few of you VERY uncomfortable with my lack of hospitality, but it just is what it is. Thankfully my girls and Jeremiah pick up my slack most of the time. The bottom line is, know who you are and give yourself grace. Is it hard for you to give yourself grace? What are the biggest things you beat yourself up over? Share them below.

DAY 10

....

....

....

....

....

....

....

....

GET TO THE ROOT

Thanks for being transparent and sharing your thoughts and feelings during the last ten days. When we start admitting we are struggling in areas, we can begin to fix them. Thank you for really digging in and investing in yourself. Speaking of digging in, let's cut to the chase and get to the root of the problem. If we want the fruit of perfectionism to quit growing and popping up in our life, then we need to get to the underlying cause and uproot it.

One day when I was having a pity party, our business and financial consultant Eric Hudson finally called me on it. I was probably going on and on about how I felt like I was never enough. I never did enough. I should be helping this person more, or that person more. This project could be better. That book should have been finished. I should have marketed that product a different way. I forgot to tell so and so happy birthday. The words he said still ring loud in my ears.

Eric: Why?

Me: What do you mean why?

Eric: Why do you feel that way?

Me: Well, because I want to help people and add value to people. I don't want people to think I don't care. I want to do my best.

Eric: Why?

Me: Why do I want to add value to people? Why do I want to do my best?

Eric: I'm not saying your answer is going to be bad. I just want to know WHY.

I sat and thought on this for a very long time. If I were to be honest, I still ask myself this question often. Why? I think a bit of it is due to pride, but I believe the majority of it is because I don't want to disappoint. When I stop and think about the one thing that crushes my spirit more than anything, it's when I feel like I let someone down. When this happens, I feel as if I didn't add value. Why is it so important for me to add value? Do I get my value from adding value? Hmm, that's a great question. Maybe I don't want to be rejected by others. I want others to accept me. If I add value, perhaps they will never deny me or reject me. I was pondering this question for several weeks in my head, and then I ran across the most amazing passage in the Bible. Take a few minutes and read chapters 17 and 18 in the Gospel of John. If you don't have a Bible, look it up online really quick. I promise it will blow your mind.

PERFECT YET REJECTED

This was a MAJOR light bulb moment for me. Jesus loved deeply. He loved with a deeper love than I have ever loved someone. Yet He was still rejected, denied, and put to death. Did you notice He was praying for His disciples one minute and then the next minute everything went south? The very people He brought alongside Him and poured His life into, denied Him. You ready for the jaw dropping moment? He was PERFECT. All of those things happened to a perfect individual. You and I will never obtain perfectionism. We are imperfect people, dealing with imperfect people. Sounds like the perfect scenario of a successful relationship, right? Many times we strive for perfection because we don't want people to get upset with us, leave us, or abandon us. Well, my friend, it happened to the only perfect individual. I hate to be the bearer of bad news, but you will let people down on this journey of life. People will let you down as well. All we can do is strive for excellence and be intentional with growing each day.

If you deal with perfectionism, let Eric's words ring in your ears. Why? From where do you think the root cause stems? Spend some time thinking this over and writing down your thoughts. When you are finished, we will close this out in prayer.

....

....

....

....

....

....

....

....

....

DAY 10

Jesus, thank you for your Word. Thank you that we can go to it and be encouraged. Give us wisdom and revelation as we read it and soak it in. Lord, I pray for all my friends who may be dealing with perfectionism. I pray they begin to find freedom from striving for something they never will be able to obtain. Open our eyes to the ways we allow it to steal our peace and joy. Help us dig down to the root cause of why we feel the need to be perfect. We are not equipped in our might to remove this from our lives, so we ask you to step in and give us freedom through your Holy Spirit. We find our value in you. We are enough in you. When we begin to compare ourselves to others, remind us of our unique designs. You did not make a mistake when you formed us. Jesus, help us be content as we walk through the different season of life. Thank you again for my friends and the time they are devoting to you. I pray they will one day look back on this season of their life and see that it was a defining season. It was a time that their lives were impacted and changed because of the time they spent with you. Jesus, you get all the glory and praise. Their lives will be a testimony for you, because of all the great things you have done. They will be world changers and leave a legacy for you. Thank you for that Jesus. Amen.

WALK IT OUT

1 Spend time thinking and meditating on the chapters of John 17 and 18.

2 Acknowledge when you are embracing perfectionism in your life. Knowing is half the battle. Write out those times in a journal and how they make you feel.

3 Give grace to yourself and others. Have unrealistic expectations hindered your relationships? Ask for forgiveness. Pray for the Lord to open your eyes when you allow this to creep back in your life.

4 Memorize and meditate on Ecclesiastes 11:4.

DAY 10

NOTES

....
....
....
....
....
....
....
....
....
....
....
....
....
....

NOTES

DAY *Eleven*
CREATIVE
PROBLEM
SOLVING

Why hello there! It's time to get down to some nuts and bolts of business. You ready??? Today we are going to talk about creative problem solving. First, let's review your accomplishments over the last several days. You have given this business over to God. You are finding freedom from your past. You have figured out your gifts and talents. You have caught a vision. You have decided to be intentional. You are growing you. You are not going to give up. You are living a life of worship. You are embracing excellence, but kicking perfectionism to the curb. That is a lot. YAY you! You may be thinking you haven't fully accomplished day so and so yet, well hang in there. We are all a work in progress. Just sit back and enjoy the journey.

OBSTACLES PROVIDE OPPORTUNITIES

Let's dive into creative problem solving, shall we? When a problem presents itself in your business, what is your very first reaction? Do you freak out? Is the sky falling? Is the end drawing near? One of the biggest tips I can give you, outside of praying for your business, is to be a creative problem solver. You should be on cloud nine when a difficult situation comes your way. Why? Simple. Now you have the chance to think of a way around it. I would dare to say the majority of my huge wins in business, have come from solutions to problems I was facing at the time. Let me explain.

Problems are what propelled me into the business I'm in today. You see, in January 2013, the company I am now working for had a promotion for free products if you ordered a certain amount that month. Insert problem. I quit my nursing job a few months before, and we had zero extra money. My husband is such a genius. He came up with a creative solution. He suggested I ask my friends if they wanted to add to my order. We wouldn't be out any money and I would get free product. Hmmm. Sounded pretty simple to me. I agreed but quickly stated that I would NEVER EVER do the business side of this company. I just wanted to use the products. We see how that worked out. Long story short. Post made. Orders received. Friends loved the product as much as I did and they wanted more. Wow, okay. So maybe I do the business. Insert problem number two. I had a business fail four years previously, and my priorities were way out of line in the midst of it. I did NOT want to walk that path again. Solution? Commit to 21 days of prayer and fasting for this new business idea. Pray for a strong foundation. Pray for vision and direction. Give control over to God. As you can see, creative problem solving was working out for me before I ever even started this new business venture.

The problems didn't stop after the 21 days of prayer was over. Nope. They kept rolling in. Remember that surprise wedding we had to go to after our car broke down? Well, as we were getting ready to head out of town, another problem arose. I had TEN members wanting to join me in this business venture, and they had loads of questions. I was still very new and had no clue how to manage it all. Jeremiah and I put our thinking caps on and within five minutes we had a solution. We decided to create a Facebook group. We put all ten members in the group. When one person asked a question, we could answer it, and the nine other people would see it too. That group ended up turning into a massive community and was a huge part of our success. Each time an obstacle came in front of us, it provided an opportunity. Every. Single. Time.

I have to tell you, 90% of the conversations Jeremiah and I have are about this very thing. How can we fix something? How can we make this better? How can this be done easier? If you want to find success in your business, then see problems and obstacles as opportunities. These issues provide the platform for you to step to the plate and be creative. The bigger the problem, the harder it will be to push through it and find a solution. Do you know what that means? The reward for your time and effort will be huge. Can you think of times when you turned problems into opportunities? Share it below.

DAY 11

....

....

....

....

....

TRY TRY AGAIN

Now hear me out, this isn't always easy. Nope. We have to think. You know what else? You may have to try one, two, three, four, maybe a million different solutions before you find one that works. So if you freak out over failure, oh boy, you better buckle up, it could be a bumpy ride. I don't like the word failure though. Failure isn't a failure if you learn something from it. You just learned that specific approach didn't work. If your idea crashes and burns, then get back up, think of another solution, and try again. Successful people get back up. Successful people try again. Successful people don't sit in a corner and cry. Successful people don't constantly complain that things are too hard.

Successful people find a problem as a challenge, and they tackle it with all their might.

RELY ON GOD

Are you freaking out right now and thinking this is way too hard? Do you believe there is no way you can do this? Good. That makes my heart happy. Why? Now you must rely on God and not you. When you are weak, then you are strong in Him. He can do immeasurably more than you can ask or imagine. You can do ALL things through Christ who strengthens you. I am 100% confident that if you ask God to help you come up with creative ideas to problems you are facing, He will give you those ideas. Maybe the idea stems from something you try that doesn't work. Remember, God's ways and thoughts are not always like our ways and thoughts, don't limit Him. Before we close out in prayer, think about some current situations you are up against in your business. Do you have some obstacles you are facing? List them out below and then let's go to the Lord in prayer over them.

....

....

....

....

....

You've got this. Actually, God's got this. We are going to pray, brainstorm, then execute an idea. If it doesn't work, repeat the steps above and start again. Right? Good, I knew you would be all over this creative problem solving and ready to go after it. Let's pray.

Jesus, you are the ultimate creative problem solver. There are things we are facing that we just can't figure out on our own. We feel like we keep hitting our head against a brick wall. We feel like we are running in circles. We are trying to come up with solutions to problems we are facing, and we just aren't getting them. Lord, show us how to conquer the issues we are facing in our businesses. We need divine wisdom from you. We need discernment from you. Give us wisdom way beyond our years. Lord, give us the confidence to try the things you prompt us to do. Give us creative ideas. Lord, we will always give you credit and point things back to you.

You can do more than we can ask or think. We don't want to do this on our own. We need your help. Show us the times we fall into the trap of complaining and grumbling. You care about each aspect of our lives. I know you care about the issues we face. Thank you for all the ideas you are going to pour out on my friends. Draw near to them as they draw near to you. We love you and thank you for all you do for us! Amen.

Below are some verses you can think on today. When you need wisdom, turn to the ONE who gives generously. I pray you have the best day ever! See you back here tomorrow!

If any of you lacks wisdom, you should ask God, who gives generously to all without finding fault, and it will be given to you.

James 1:5 (NIV)

For the Lord gives wisdom; from his mouth come knowledge and understanding.

Proverbs 2:6 (NIV)

DAY 11

WALK IT OUT

1 When you catch yourself complaining about a problem, stop and think of a solution instead. Ask the Lord to help you have wisdom and discernment on how to handle the situation.

2 Ask tons of questions. Find out what the needs are in your business. What are the issues, struggles, and problems? Work with others to find resolutions.

3 Find a quiet place to sit and think. Think every single day.

4 Memorize and meditate on 2 Corinthians 12:10, Ephesians 3:20, Philippians 4:13, James 1:5, and Proverbs 2:6.

NOTES

DAY *Twelve*
BUILD COMMUNITY

Day Twelve. You keep coming back for more. I LOVE IT! Did you solve all your business issues yesterday with your creative problem solving? You can have another day or two if you need more. I'll cut you some slack. Today is going to be a fun topic, actually a critical topic. We are going to discuss the importance of building community. The Bible clearly states we need to meet together. There is also a mission given to us to accomplish during these times together. Let's check it out below.

> And let us consider how we may spur one another on toward love and good deeds, not giving up meeting together, as some are in the habit of doing, but encouraging one another—and all the more as you see the Day approaching.

Hebrews 10:24-25 (NIV)

Do not give up meeting together. Well, that seems pretty straightforward to me, how about you? We are better together. I am sure you have heard that saying before. It is so true. Doing "life" with others and not alone brings great rewards. When we meet together and do life together, we can spur one another on toward love and good deeds. We can bring encouragement to one another. Being alone is, well, lonely. Being alone is also very dangerous. Let me prove it to you.

THERE'S SAFETY IN NUMBERS

Have you ever seen one of those shows filmed on the African savanna? You know, the one where the lion is chasing a group of gazelles? OH. MY. WORD. Your heart is racing, and your adrenaline is kicked up to crazy level. RUN GAZELLES, RUN! You want to look away, but you can't. Then all of the sudden it happens. One gazelle gets outside the safety of that big massive group. Not good. You know the rest of the story. Look away. Look away. I like to think those gazelles are encouraging each other along. I have a vivid imagination. Just play along with me. Can't you hear them yelling at each other? Run Gail the gazelle. You can do it, stick with us. Don't give up. Make those legs work faster Gary the gazelle. Glenda the gazelle, you are good. I can see Larry the lion way behind us. Keep running.

I know, I know, that's probably not how it goes down. It should be how it goes down in the communities we build, though. Am I right, or am I right? The race of life is challenging. We need to have people running alongside us that are encouraging us to keep on keeping on. We need to be encouraging others to do the same. When you are alone and facing tough times, it's hard to see the light at the end of the tunnel. Remember my story of that fateful day in February? I needed the encouragement of my friends. Share a time or two below where a friend or a community helped you make it through a tough time. Can you think of times where you helped others when they were at their lowest? Share that as well.

....

....

....

....

....

DON'T STICK TO THE SIDELINES

Encouragement comes in more ways than just one. Many times we think of encouragement as just helping someone through a hard time. While that *is* encouragement, we can also encourage others with the life we live. Yep. We can spur each other towards love and good deeds as we embrace love and good deeds in our lives. I recently watched a news report of an amazing way a teenage boy brought joy to a young little girl. These little girls who were cheerleaders were having a special ceremony at halftime of a football game. Their fathers came out on the field and lifted them each on their shoulders, all except one little girl. Her father had just been stationed overseas and wasn't there. While all the dads stood there holding their little girls, this little girl begins to cry. It was too much for her to handle. She missed her daddy so much. Out of nowhere, a teenage boy sees what is happening. He is shocked; no one is running to her side. He leaves the bleachers, jumps the fence, runs and scoops up the little girl and lifts her to his shoulders. I was ugly face crying as I sat and watched. His good deed encouraged me. He encouraged me to be mindful of others. His good deed inspired me not just to sit on the sidelines of life observing, but to jump the fence and do something about it. Have you been inspired by the good deeds of others? If so, share a few ways below.

....

....

....

DAY 12

WHAT KEEPS YOU FROM COMMUNITY

I think you and I both agree communities are important. If we believe they are important, why are we hesitant to be part of one? Why do we stand on the outside looking in and get a little sick to our stomach? Wait, has that only happened to me? Surely you have dealt with these feelings too. Oh, my friends, I know these feelings far too well. Maybe you have been part of a group and got your feelings hurt. Have you been rejected by others? Did someone let you down? Did you vow never to let that happen again? This is why it is so important to walk in freedom from your past. Hurts happen. Those harms continue to hurt you if you refuse to move forward. What if it happens again? It may. That's a risk you're going to have to take. Don't allow these pains to keep you from all the great things that may come your way. Let me tell you how this went down for me.

There was a day when I vowed I would never be friends with another girl. Sorry girls, no offense, but we can be mean. For four years I lived up to that vow. I had my surface friendships, and that was it. We went to a large church that encouraged you to be part of small groups, and I wanted nothing of it. I checked one or two out and justified not going because of how busy I was with work and taking care of my girls. Not joining in seemed like a safe choice to me. This highly insecure girl was about to find freedom, though. In October 2012, I was driving to a women's retreat at our church. I remember right where I was on the interstate when Kelli Wright called me. I knew her, but we were not close friends. She wanted to know if we could sit together. OK, why not. Might as well. It was that conference where I found freedom from those past hurts. I told God I was done being a slave to those feelings. I was tired and worn down. That night I not only found freedom, but I found a new community that was about to begin.

Are you fearful of being part of a community? Have you been hurt before? If so, share your feelings below. I really do appreciate you being open and transparent.

DAY 12

....

....

....

....

....

....

....

HANG ON THERE'S HOPE

Don't let reliving all those memories get you down. There is hope. Tomorrow we are going to dive into the subject of conflict and how you survive it. For now, let's keep on with the subject of community. If you are willing to give this whole community and friend thing another try, where do you begin? How do you build a community? Where do you start? Great questions. Start with what is currently in front of you. That night when I found freedom from all those hurts, I put action to my prayers. I asked Kelli if she wanted to start meeting once a week just to hang out and chat. I had two other girls in mind I wanted to ask as well. We began meeting up that very next week, and we formed a beautiful community of four friends. Those three girls, Kelli, Anna, and Natalie, were the girls who encouraged me on that February day to never give up. You remember the story, right? Can you see how my past hurts could have kept me from the future encouragement I would one day need? Does that mean I haven't faced hard times since finding freedom? Wish I could tell you it's been smooth sailing since that day in October. I can tell you one thing; I wouldn't go back and do anything differently.

So talk to me. How could you start building community with what is currently in front of you? Do you have friendships that could be made stronger? Are you part of a church or small group that meets weekly? Do you have a hobby you enjoy that has Facebook groups you could join? List some ways below that you can get involved or start a community yourself.

DAY 12

....

....

....

....

....

....

....

Let's read one more verse that shows why embracing friendships and community is important.

> As iron sharpens iron, so a friend sharpens a friend.
>
> *Proverbs 27:17 (NLT)*

See, you need your friend and your friend also needs you. Together you make one another stronger. Let's pray.

Father, we love you so very much. Thank you for speaking to us through your Word. Thank you for showing us the importance of community and friendships. Lord, we want to build friendships, but most importantly, we want you to be part of those bonds. Help us find friends and a community of people who are seeking after you, who want to know your ways and walk in those ways. I pray right now Jesus for all those who have been hurt and fearful of trying this whole friend thing again. I pray you give them peace and comfort in knowing you are a friend that sticks closer than a brother. They may be hurt time and time again, but you will never abandon them. I pray you bring friends into their life for such a time as this. Jesus, I pray they find encouragement and spur one another along in love and good deeds. I thank you in advance for birthing beautiful things out of these friendships. I know you have big things in store. Thank you Jesus. Amen.

WALK IT OUT

1 Call a friend and set up a lunch date. If you want bonus points, find a friend you haven't connected with in a while. You know you want bonus points.

2 Start a group text or group message with a couple of your closest friends. Make a point to stay connected throughout the week.

3 Put your creative thinking cap on and find ways to build community in your business. This can be done in person or through social media. Embrace what works best for you in your current situation.

4 Memorize and meditate on Hebrews 10:24-25 and Proverbs 27:17.

DAY 12

NOTES

DAY 12

NOTES

DAY *Thirteen*
SURVIVING CONFLICT

F ancy meeting you here again. It thrills me that you keep coming back day after day. I'm just warning you before we start. I have some good news and some bad news. Today's topic is something you are going to need to read, then read again, then read again, and then read again. Why? Because the topic is about conflict, and for the love of everything, conflict is something we ALL have faced. If you have not faced conflict, you must be on a deserted island all by yourself. Once you remove yourself from seclusion, be warned, you will face conflict on the rest of your journey through life. That's the bad news. Let me bring you some good news. You can survive conflict. I know you are screaming liar, liar, pants on fire, but it's true. I am not telling you it will be fun, but you can survive it. Ready to dive in? Game on!

Once you give God control, find freedom, discover your unique design, gain vision, become intentional, grow, never give up, live a life of worship, embrace excellence, kick perfectionism to the curb, become a creative problem solver, and build a community, it's not all rainbows and unicorns from that point forward. It may seem like it for a period of time, but that's until conflict steps in (insert dramatic music). It was bound to happen. The moment you feared. The day you never wanted to see. Conflict happens way more than we want to admit, and we need to know how to handle it. Our goal is to take care of it and make it to the other side in one piece.

VERY FEW PEOPLE WAKE UP EVIL

Okay, let's start a tough subject by visiting a Pixar movie. Seems logical, right? Have you ever watched the movie UP? Isn't it so good? If you haven't seen it, I am about to give you some spoilers, be warned. I want to tell you a little something I took away from the movie. This story opened my eyes to a new way of viewing conflict. I hope it gives you a new perspective as well.

In the opening scene of the movie, they give you a quick overview of the life of Carl Fredricksen. He is a little boy that met a little girl named Ellie. You see the story unfold of how they played together as kids. They fell in love, got married, faced hard times, even the loss of a child, had dreams of adventure, they grow old together, then we see the end stages of Ellie's life, then death. Mr. Fredricksen is now alone. Not only is he alone, he feels like he let the love of his life down. They never were able to go on that adventure she had dreams of experiencing. He is facing deep hurt and pain. In the midst of this pain, he has another problem. New buildings are going up all around his little house that he and Ellie lived in their whole life. Construction crews want to tear his house down and build new buildings. He just can't let it go. This was their home. He felt like all he had left of Ellie was here in this house. People thought he was crazy. They thought he was this mean old man. The next scene is where my eyes were opened to see others in a different light.

One morning the construction crews were working around his house. Mr. Fredricksen walks out just about the time a truck backs over his mailbox. This mailbox was special, it had the handprints he and Ellie put on there the day they moved into the house. As I was watching this, I could feel my heart begin to burst with sadness. His heart was already hurting, and now this made the pain unbearable. Ellie was gone, now the physical memories they created together were being destroyed right before his eyes. Mr. Fredricksen loses it. The grumpy old man who had never lashed out and hurt others despite his pain lifted up his cane and hit the driver across the head. The man begins to bleed. People are looking on in shock. What is this man's problem? He must be an evil old man. What a horrible person. Mr. Fredricksen immediately realizes what he has just done. He hangs his head down and goes back inside his house. I am sure he was ashamed.

Why do we look at Mr. Fredricksen differently than those who were standing around when he hit this driver? Why do others look on in disbelief, while we shed a tear? Why do we have sympathy, while others want to make him pay for his wrong doings? You know the answer to those questions. We are aware of his backstory. We are conscious of his hurts. We understand. Did you know this same story plays out in front of us each and every day? We stand on the sidelines and shake our heads in disbelief that others are lashing out and hurting one another. What is their problem? Why are they so grumpy? What is the deal? Why are they so rude? We for a brief moment forget, people who are hurting, tend to hurt others. Or, as I've often heard it said, hurting people hurt people. We forget they may have a backstory.

Can I throw a question your way? Do you feel like you can relate to Mr. Fredricksen? Maybe his story is your story. Your spirit is crushed. Your hurt is deep. You feel alone. When Mr. Fredricksen hit that driver, you could see the expression on his face immediately change. He went from being angry to being embarrassed. He didn't set out to hurt that man that day. It was a reaction out of his pain. He was hurting, and he reacted with hurt. Have you experienced that too? Have you ever hurt someone and it was done out of a deep-rooted pain or insecurity you were dealing with in your life? If you feel comfortable, do you mind writing it out in the space provided?

....
....
....
....
....

Can I ask you one more question? Have you ever felt like you let someone down? Mr. Fredricksen not only felt the pain of losing Ellie, he felt like he failed her in life. Have you experienced that feeling? If you have watched the movie, you know Ellie didn't feel he let her down. At the end of the film, Mr. Fredricksen finds a scrapbook that tells of their life together. Ellie tells him their life together was her greatest adventure. The one thing that stole his joy, his possible failure, never actually existed. Whether we have let someone down or it's just something we are making up in our minds, it can weigh us down. That heavy weight leaves us insecure. Those insecurities can come to the surface and cause hurt to others and ourselves. I know you thought you were going to get out of writing on this subject, but I can't allow you not to visit this today. Can you think of examples of this in your life? Can you think of times when you felt like you let others down? Share it below if you don't mind.

....
....
....
....
....

I believe the number one way to survive conflict, is first to understand all we talked about above. Ask the Lord to give you a heart for the other person. Ask to see their hurts. Ask to figure out why they have done the things they have done. Next, we need to examine ourselves. Conflict is typically a two-way street. I know the things I've faced, I played a part in the conflict. Whether I intentionally meant to or not, it's the truth. Many times we give ourselves much more grace than we are willing to give others. We want people to look past our failures, but we will never allow them to live down the hurts they have brought to us. We need help from God on this, let's go to His Word.

DAY 13

A new command I give you: Love one another. As I have loved you, so you must love one another. By this everyone will know that you are my disciples, if you love one another.

John 13:34-35 (NIV)

Love the Lord your God with all your heart and with all your soul and with all your mind. This is the first and greatest commandment. And the second is like it: Love your neighbor as yourself.

Matthew 22:37-39 (NIV)

Anyone who claims to be in the light but hates a brother or sister is still in the darkness. Anyone who loves their brother and sister lives in the light, and there is nothing in them to make them stumble.

1 John 2:9-10 (NIV)

Memorize these verses. Meditate on these verses. Pray these verses over your life. Ask the Lord to help you love others as you love yourself. Ask the Lord to help you love others the way He loves them. On that note, let's close in prayer.

Jesus, conflict is a topic that touches deep into the hearts of so many reading today. Lord, you know their hurts and disappointments. You know how conflict has paralyzed them and kept them from being who you made them to be. I am sure many are afraid to trust and get close to someone again. Today, I pray they break through that Jesus. We need you to help us with conflict. Relational issues are one of the hardest things to work through. That is why WE NEED you. Jesus, reveal to us ways we can interact with others in a healthy manner. Jesus, help us love others the way you love us. Give us a heart for others, a heart for those who may have done us wrong. Help us have sympathy, understanding, grace and mercy. Help us see where the root of the issues come from, and how we can fix it. I pray again for peace for all those who have a heavy heart and those who have been hurt. Jesus, today, let them walk away with such a peace and joy in their hearts. Give them confidence you have got this under control. Help us love others the way you love them. May we not focus on all the faults of others, but rather the hurts the others may be experiencing. Let us see them through your eyes. Please speak to the hearts of everyone reading this today. We need you. We love you so much. Amen.

DAY 13

WALK IT OUT

1 We mentioned studying personality types earlier in our time together. I would like you to visit it again. It is important to understand how you and others are wired. It will open your eyes to how quickly misunderstandings can take place. Remember, very few people wake up evil.

2 Take time to pause and reflect when you are presented with something that ruffles your feathers. Give yourself time to cool down. This almost ALWAYS brings about a better response.

3 Concealing your feelings by brushing them under the rug can be very dangerous. Nasty things grow in the dark. They are only hidden for a while. The minute you snap, it's going to get ugly, FAST. The hard conversations now will never be as painful or hurtful as what happens when an explosion occurs.

4 Memorize and meditate on John 13:34-35, Matthew 22:37-39, and 1 John 2:9-10.

NOTES

DAY 13

NOTES

DAY 13

NOTES

DAY *Fourteen*

FIGHT FOR
YOUR FAMILY

W hat? Is it day fourteen already? Have we been walking through this together for two whole weeks? There is no stopping you now. You are in this thing to the END. I am so proud of you for sticking it out and allowing the Lord to have HIS way in your life and business. We have been handing things over to God, finding freedom, figuring out how we are uniquely made, catching visions, being intentional, growing, not quitting, living a life of worship, doing things with excellence, being free of perfectionism, creative problem solving, building communities, and surviving conflicts. We are accomplishing some great things with God's help in our lives and businesses. Let's make sure to fight for our families with the same tenacity.

I would love to tell you that I'm an expert in the "family" department, but that's just not the case. Jeremiah and I love each other and our girls very much. However, trust me, we have our moments. Don't we all? I never want to paint a picture that my family is perfect and lives the fairytale life. We have our issues. No matter what your family life looks like, there is always room to make it better. Be intentional. Wouldn't you agree?

I need to let you in on a little secret. I love to work. A LOT. Well, at least the kind of work that's embracing who I was made to be. It's hard for me even to call it work. I love what I do. I can talk about work 24/7. I can talk about you 24/7. I can dream up ideas 24/7. I love to dream. Many times I feel like my family is getting kicked to the curb in the middle of all this work. I deal with tons of guilt when this happens. I am sure I'm not alone, right? Have you ever had guilt hit you like a ton of bricks? I think we all need to be mindful and fight for our families. However, I do feel like we need to give a little grace and mercy to ourselves.

Remember what we said about excellence vs. perfectionism? I believe many times we allow comparison to creep into our personal lives, just as we do in our businesses. We look at what we think the "perfect" family portrays, and we strive for that same family. We never obtain it. We only see our faults and our shortcomings. Comparison steals your joy no matter what's being compared. Have you fallen prey to comparison in this area of your life? Have you seen families and thought if you could just have it all together as they do, your life would be perfect? You know what I'm about to ask you to do, don't you? Do you mind writing some of those times out? I know I'm asking some very personal questions. I pray the time you spend thinking on this will open your eyes to things you can bring to the Lord in prayer for today.

....

....

....

....

....

....

....

I believe to have a healthy and prosperous business; it helps to have a healthy and thriving family. If your family life is chaotic, it spills over into your business. If your business is chaotic, it spills over into your family. How do you have a healthy and thriving family? You fight for it. You embrace the same concepts we have been talking about in the *21 Days Of Prayer For Your Business* and apply it to your family. You give God control, you find freedom from your past hurts and failures, you figure out how you ALL are uniquely made, catch a VISION for your family, be INTENTIONAL with your family, find ways that everyone can grow in your family, don't give up when times get tough, let your love for your family be worship to the Lord, embrace excellence in your family, don't be a slave to perfectionism, be a creative problem solver concerning issues in your family, let your family be a community where you encourage each other daily, and understand where the root of conflict comes from inside your family unit. The Lord wants to have control over every aspect of your life. If He wants to have His way in your business, you know He wants to help you in the area of your family. Ask for His help. Pray for a stronger family.

I believe it's time I air some dirty laundry. Recently, Jeremiah and I went to IKEA for some office furniture and returned with a trip to Hawaii. How is that airing dirty laundry? Oh, wait for the story, you are about to find out. Let me set the stage for you. The characters are Monique and Jeremiah McLean. Both individuals are extremely strong willed and very opinionated. The location is a small section in the corner of IKEA, a mockup office area to be exact. Currently, the two have been working together 24/7 for almost two years straight. Their topic of conversation consists of business 99.9% of that time. Now is where it gets heated. As Jeremiah and I stood in IKEA, our love for each other was taken over by a fit of rage. It was over something critical to the existence of all mankind, wait for it, a FILING CABINET. Yep. World War III was going down, and everyone around us knew it. I'm not even clear now what we were arguing about, but it ended with us both walking out and leaving with no furniture.

As we were driving down the road, I realized how silly it was to be fighting over a filing cabinet. I put my creative problem-solving hat on and started thinking. First, what was the root issue here? It was NOT the filing cabinet. It had to be something deeper. We weren't having any fun together, what was the deal? Wait, when was the last time we had a conversation about something other than business? When was the last time we went on a trip just the two of us? My creative problem solving got kicked up into high gear and I picked up my phone and called Delta. We had credits from a trip we had to cancel a few weeks back and there you have it, free flights to Hawaii. Score. We left in less than 48 hours to spend seven nights just the two of us. I must be honest with you, we still did a little work. It's way more romantic working from a lounge chair. Sometimes you have to stop the craziness of your business and fight for your family. It's worth it. It doesn't have to be a trip to Hawaii. It can be traveling one city over. It can be simply shutting your computer and finding a movie to snuggle on the couch and watch. The point is, be intentional. Make time for your family. What are ways you create intentional family time?

....

....

....

....

....

I'm not sure what your family dynamic looks like, but we have two girls who are in their teenage years. We try so hard to make this our journey, a family journey. This is not a Monique journey, or my mom and dad's journey, but our journey. We are a family. We have walked through some MAJOR hard times together, and we have walked through some great times together. We have done a lot of things wrong, but one thing I can say, we have FOUGHT for our family. I look at my family often and realize it doesn't look like the typical family. We aren't settled down in one place. We travel a ton. It seems chaotic most of the time, but it's our family. When perfectionism and comparison creep in, I just have to pray we are walking out excellence in what is put before us.

What happens if you are single? Great question. Learn these principles now. If you do plan on getting married and having kids, these will be tools you can use down the road. If you aren't married, you still have a family. What about your parents, brothers or sisters, extended family? Fight for a strong relationship with them. Many times friends are as close as family. Fight for strong relationships there too. When it's all said and done, family nine times out of ten have your back. They are usually WAY more forgiving than the rest of the world out there. They are with you to the end. Let's not take what we have lightly. Let's be intentional. Let's devote it to God. Let's FIGHT FOR IT. Let's pray...

Jesus, we love you. Lord, I thank you for yet another day that people took time out to devote to you. Jesus, today we ask you to have your way in the lives of our families. We need you! Lord, help us not get so caught up in our work, in being busy, that we neglect those who are most important to us, family. Show us ways we can grow closer to one another. Show us ways our families can interact in our businesses. Show us how you uniquely made each of our family members. Help us to catch a vision for our family. Help us grow. Help us be intentional. Lord, if some people reading today feel like they have NO family, remind them that you are their Heavenly Father. Show them ways they can get connected in a community to find family. Jesus, I pray for those who have major battle scars when it comes to the topic of family. I have no clue what those reading this have faced over the years, but you know. Lord, I ask you heal areas of their lives that need healing. Relational issues are hard, but relational issues inside the family can be earth shattering. Lord, pull pieces back together. Restore relationships. Bring peace. We want to be thriving in all areas of our lives. We can't do this on our own. We need you. We will fight for our families, but we want your help. Jesus, again, I love you so much. Pour out your blessings on those who are devoting this time to seeking after you. Amen.

Here are a few verses for you to think about today.

Train up a child in the way he should go: and when he is old, he will not depart from it.

Proverbs 22:6 (KJV)

...but as for me and my house, we will serve the Lord.

Joshua 24:15 (ESV)

Today finished up week two. I would love for you to take some time and write out what you learned this week. Did the Lord open your eyes to certain things? Were there topics that stood out to you? Did you feel like you found freedom over things that held you captive? Share a bit in the space provided, and I will see you back here tomorrow.

....

....

....

....

....

....

....

....

....

....

....

....

....

....

....

....

WALK IT OUT

1   Be intentional and create family time. Consider this time a non-negotiable. Put it on the calendar and never let anything stand in the way.

2   Commit to putting your phones away at dinner or when you are spending devoted time with your family.

3   Start a group text or group message with your family and keep the conversation going.

4   Memorize and meditate on Proverbs 22:6 and Joshua 24:15.

DAY 14

NOTES

NOTES

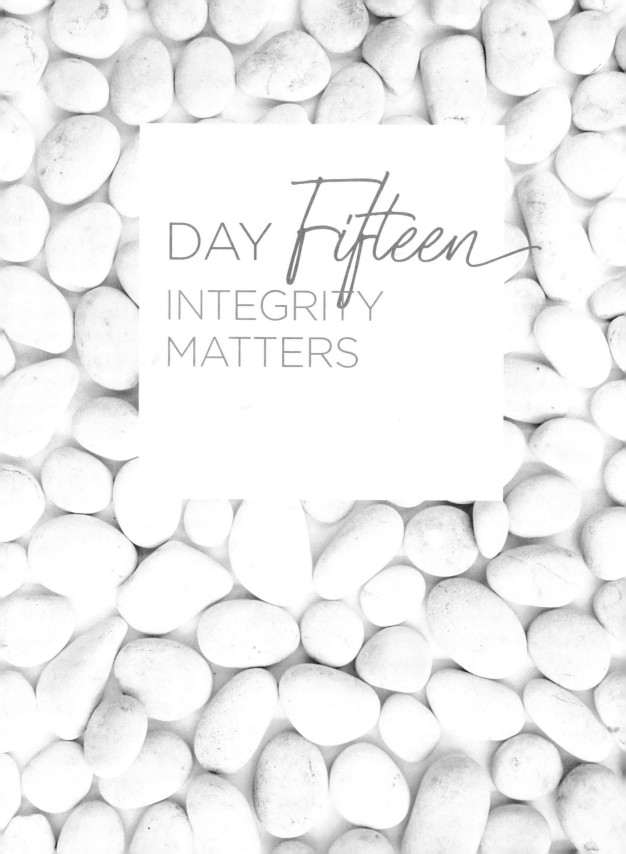

DAY *Fifteen*
INTEGRITY MATTERS

Welcome to the beginning of week three. We have covered so many different topics during our time together. We have sought after God. We have searched deep into our hearts. We have been open and honest about issues we face. I pray you have a new fresh vision for the direction of your business. I pray momentum has developed and you are encouraged like never before. I pray you are personally growing and seeing the fruit from that growth. Finally, I pray you are guarding your heart and embracing integrity in all you do. Our topic today is just that, Integrity Matters. Each day, I believe that day's topic is one of the best we have discussed. Today proves no different. Having integrity in all we do is vital for our success and peace of mind. How would you define INTEGRITY in your words?

....

....

....

....

WHAT IS INTEGRITY

Let's take a look at the definitions of integrity.

1. *A firm adherence to a code of especially moral or artistic values.*
2. *The quality or state of being complete or undivided.*

Did you notice that first definition? Read it one more time.

• *A firm adherence to a code of especially moral or artistic VALUES.*

We have talked about our values a good bit during the 21 days of prayer. It is important to KNOW your values. When you aren't getting your values into your day, you don't feel balanced. You are probably frustrated. INTERESTING. Read what the second definition says about integrity.

• *The quality or state of being complete or undivided.*

By permission. From Merriam-Webster's Collegiate® Dictionary, 11th Edition ©2016 by MerriamWebster, Inc.

I had a light bulb moment when thinking about these definitions. I always think of INTEGRITY as being honest and not telling a lie. Yes, integrity means just that, it falls under moral values. However, think of it a different way. We feel division in our lives when we have strong values, and we aren't embracing them in all we do. We just don't feel complete. Having integrity in your business is about being honest and faithful to you and your values as much as it is about being truthful and honest in your business dealings. BOTH are equally important.

Integrity is doing the honorable thing no matter what. Integrity is doing the right thing when nobody else is watching you. Integrity is not taking a dishonest shortcut. Integrity is taking the high road, even though it may be harder to walk. Integrity is crucial in every situation. Why? Once you compromise integrity, even in the smallest way, it's easier and easier to compromise again and again. It is SO important to embrace integrity in every single thing you do. It sets the tone of your business. I look at integrity as being a foundation. A person who has integrity in all they do has a strong foundation. They are firm, stable, and reliable. When you begin to compromise a little here and there, it gets easier to compromise later. The strong foundation you have built starts to crumble. To be fruitful and thriving in all we do, we MUST keep that strong.

COST OF COMPROMISE

I notice a trend when I look back over the course of my life and see the times I had real hard failures. Many of those times were because of a lack of integrity in my decisions and business practices. There are no shortcuts worth taking in your business. Don't fall into that trap. Integrity matters. It matters in your everyday life, and it matters in your business. When times are tough, integrity is vital. Tough and turbulent times are when you need to be on guard. These times are the easiest to compromise your integrity and to take those shortcuts. Don't do it. When times are tough for your business, you feel like you are grasping for anything to make it better. Being dishonest and compromising your values is not the answer. It may seem like the logical thing to do at the time, but it will only sink you into deeper trouble. You can never go wrong embracing integrity.

Here's the time where I turn it over to you. Can you think of times in your life when integrity took the backseat? Have you ever compromised your values? How did that turn out? How did it make you feel? Before you begin to share your thoughts, let's chat about something. When we go through these times where we dig deep into our lives, please guard your heart. These questions are not meant to bring condemnation upon your life. We all have made mistakes.

We all have regrets. We all have compromised our values at some point. Please don't allow our times of reflecting to weigh you down. Now that you have promised not to be hard on yourself, you can begin to share your thoughts below.

....

....

....

....

Here is what the Bible says about integrity.

> For the Lord grants wisdom! From his mouth come knowledge and understanding. He grants a treasure of common sense to the honest. He is a shield to those who walk with integrity.
>
> *Proverbs 2:6-7 (NLT)*

> The integrity of the upright guides them, but the crookedness of the treacherous destroys them.
>
> *Proverbs 11:3 (ESV)*

> The godly walk with integrity; blessed are their children who follow them.
>
> *Proverbs 20:7 (NLT)*

When we keep integrity in all that we do, I honestly believe the Lord is watching out for us. He has our back. When we make the right choices, even when nobody is watching, the Lord sees our hearts. He sees that we are walking in integrity. It's not worth it to cut corners. One little compromise today grows into bigger compromises down the road. We have a rule in our house regarding our money and taxes. If it is questionable, we don't do it. It's not worth the ramifications that come from being dishonest. I am positive the Lord blesses our honesty. There was a day when we cut corners. We didn't walk with as much integrity. That business didn't turn out well for us. You can never, ever, ever go wrong walking in integrity.

Remember our talk about excellence? We will never be perfect, but we can strive to be better and better each day. Ask the Lord to prompt you when things are questionable. Ask Him to open your eyes and give you wisdom and discernment. Ask others to hold you accountable. Find friends who will ask you the hard questions. These things will get you moving in the right direction. On that note, let's pray.

Jesus, we love you. We want so desperately to know your ways and walk in them. We want to embrace integrity in all we do. Lord, help us to hold true to the values you have set deep in our hearts. May we NEVER waiver in those values. We want to maintain HONESTY and INTEGRITY in every single thing we do, even the smallest of details. Jesus, show us when we start to take shortcuts. We don't want to compromise and take the easy path. We want a strong foundation. We want this in our daily lives and our businesses. Jesus, when times get tough, when times are hard, help us embrace integrity even stronger. We don't want one little decision or compromise to lead to another and another. We need your help. Our flesh wants to get in the way. We need you. Be quick to speak to our hearts when we compromise. Point out the areas we need to work. Again, Jesus we want to Know your ways and walk in them. We love you Jesus. Amen.

WALK IT OUT

1   **Find someone who embraces integrity in their life and encourage them today. Let them know how their life inspires you. I know this will bless them.**

2   **Find a friend you can trust who will hold you accountable and ask you hard questions. Be open and honest. Share your struggles with this friend.**

3   **Keep reviewing your values and make sure they are honored in your business. When hard times come your way, embrace them even stronger.**

4   **Memorize and meditate on Proverbs 2:6-7, Proverbs 11:3, and Proverbs 20:7.**

NOTES

DAY *Sixteen*
BE
COURAGEOUS

Hello, hello! Did reading today's topic give you a case of butterflies in your stomach? It takes courage to be courageous. Wait is that even possible? That's something to think about for a bit. If you had the courage to be courageous, would that mean you were already courageous? That's too much for my mind to think about, let's just jump right in and get started. How would you define the word courageous in your own words? Write it out below, pretty please.

....

....

....

....

....

Let's look at the definition of courageous.

•   *The act of having courage*

Well okay then, how about the definition of courage?

•   *The ability to do something that you know is difficult or dangerous.*

Oh boy, here we go. We are about to live on the wild side. GAME ON. This is going to be the best day ever. Don't be scared. We are going to make it through this together.

Think of how much we have accomplished so far with God's help. We have handed things over to Him, found freedom, discovered our unique design, caught a vision, become intentional, embraced growth, decided to not give up, allowed our lives to be lived out in worship to Him, walked out excellence, found freedom over perfectionism, become creative problem solvers, built communities, survived conflicts, fought for our family, walked with integrity, now it's time to BE COURAGEOUS. Did any of those topics we cover force you into being courageous? Could it have been building community? What about dealing with conflicts? Take a second and write them out in the space provided and then give yourself a high five for having courage.

By permission. From Merriam-Webster's Collegiate® Dictionary, 11th Edition ©2016 by MerriamWebster, Inc.

....

....

....

....

....

I believe it took courage for you to pursue these 21 days of prayer. When I walked through this in January of 2016 with my friends on social media, many messaged me saying they were nervous to commit. What if they couldn't be consistent? Many had never even prayed before. Some people vowed never to have anything to do with God; they felt abandoned by Him and hurt by other Christians. There were even a few who felt like embracing God could be bad for their business. Wouldn't that cost them down the road? Would people think they were crazy? Would it offend others? Would they turn into an individual who talked about Jesus 24/7? I heard all of those concerns loud and clear. You may have even had some of the very same concerns. If so, will you share a few of them below?

....

....

....

....

....

....

COMFORT ZONE COUCH

I am so glad you stepped into your fears by walking out things that were difficult for you. Let's step into even more fears. Are you up for it? It's time we get off the comfort zone couch and start doing some things that scare us. It may be hard, but I believe in you. When we step out and do things that scare us, we grow. It forces us to rely on God more than ourselves. That is a beautiful place to be. When we are weak, HE is strong. Times like this keep us humble. Ask the Lord to present opportunities like these that will make you grow. When the doors open, walk through them. Live on the wild side. He will equip you for whatever He puts before you. Trust me; I know this first hand.

I have had to live out what I'm telling you over the last three years. Still to this day, I have to find courage. When I told the Lord back in January 2013 that I would walk through any door He opened, and point others to Him; I had no clue He was going to kick it up to crazy level so fast. I sincerely meant the words I prayed. I wasn't remembering the verse about His ways being higher than our ways. I thought I would tell a few of my friends about Him, but instead, a door opened for me to speak to a room of almost 10,000 friends. Oh, wait. I can't do that. Me? Hold up. Do you remember a couple of months back Lord, when I was standing in front of 300 and just had to say my name? My legs were shaking uncontrollably. Lord, I am not equipped to talk in front of that many people. After a bit of arguing with God, I gave in and kept my promise. I would love to tell you it was easy once I agreed to walk through that door. It wasn't though. We are talking, OH MY WORD, WHAT AM I DOING? My hands were sweaty, my mouth was like cotton and my legs were like noodles. Guess what? I survived.

That experience did several things for me. It proved to me His ways are pretty huge. It allowed me the opportunity to do what I said I would do. I made sure to let those 10,000 people know my secret to success was Jesus. It made me rely on Him. I have never prayed as much in my life as I did leading up to this event. It reminded me how faithful my Jesus is to walk by my side. It made me dream bigger. It made me overflow with gratitude for the journey I was on. He confirmed when we put Him first, He does more than we could ask or think. It was by far the scariest thing I have ever done, and I would do it all over again in a heartbeat.

What is it for you? What scares you in your business? What does stepping out of your comfort zone look like in your life? Share a few examples below.

....

....

....

....

This road of being courageous will be hard. It will prove to be difficult. Many are afraid to walk it. You, my friend, are not that person. Why? You know what you have been praying for. You know how big our God is. You know He designed you for great and mighty things. You know you were born for such a time as this. You are going to look at your fears and say, BRING IT ON! Before we close in prayer for the day, I would like to leave you some verses on being courageous.

DAY 16

For God has not given us a spirit of fear, but of power and of love and of a sound mind.

2 Timothy 1:7 (NKJV)

Have I not commanded you? Be strong and courageous. Do not be afraid; do not be discouraged, for the Lord your God will be with you wherever you go.

Joshua 1:9 (NIV)

So do not fear, for I am with you; do not be dismayed, for I am your God. I will strengthen you and help you; I will uphold you with my righteous right hand.

Isaiah 41:10 (NIV)

How amazing are these verses? I encourage you to read them over and over. Meditate on them. Memorize these verses and hide them in your heart. When times come for you to be courageous, quote these verses. Speak these verses over your life. Pray these verses over your life. We have nothing to fear because God is on our side. Let's pray.

Father, we come to you today, thanking you for all the wonderful things you have done in our lives. We thank you for drawing near to us as we draw near to you. We are grateful you never leave us or forsake us. When we step into fears, out of our comfort zone, you are right there with us. We will be COURAGEOUS. We will have COURAGE to do the things that look WAY bigger than what our human minds think we can do. We will have COURAGE to walk through the doors that you open for us. We will have the courage to say YES to the things you put before us. Jesus, these things are HARD, DIFFICULT, many times SCARY, but LORD, we know that you are strong when we are weak. That is when you work best when we don't have it all going on, and we give you room to work. Jesus, we have FAITH. We have COURAGE because we have FAITH in you. We know you will sustain us. We know you will work through us. We know you can do CRAZY AMAZING THINGS. Jesus, we want to grow in this area, so we pray that you open doors for us. Bring things our way that will push us, grow us, and FORCE us to be COURAGEOUS. We may not trust ourselves, and rightfully so, but we do trust you. We love you Jesus, OH SO MUCH. We thank you for this journey you have us all on. We are having the time of our lives. Amen.

WALK IT OUT

1 Think about times in your life when you embraced courage. What emotions did that bring in your life? Did it make you stronger? Reflect on times you have already walked through and let those inspire you.

2 Attempt one thing that scares you. Put yourself out there and trust God to help you walk through the process. I believe in you. You can do this.

3 Share with a friend the areas you feel you are complacent. Tell them your fears and allow them to encourage you as you become courageous.

4 Memorize and meditate on 2 Timothy 1:7, Joshua 1:9, and Isaiah 41:10.

NOTES

....

....

....

....

....

....

....

....

....

....

....

....

NOTES

DAY 16

NOTES

DAY *Seventeen*
BE STILL

Can we just look at that title and let out a huge sigh of relief? BE STILL. Over the last 16 days, we have had a LOT going on. We have covered many topics, dug deep into our past, thought about our struggles, and wrote out our feelings. We have put forth effort each day and carved out time to devote to this study and prayer. We have memorized verses, meditated on verses, and prayed verses over our lives and others. All of this is good and very much needed. However, we can't neglect the need for being still. If you only knew how God's timing is perfect for this subject in my life, let me explain.

MIND GAMES

When I began writing this day's topic, I had some issues hit me pretty hard. The punch went right to my biggest insecurities. Here are the thoughts that went through my mind. You are not enough Monique. You let people down Monique. You don't love enough Monique. You have failed Monique. What makes you think you can write a book that touches on topics you struggle with in life? You aren't qualified for this type of work Monique. You've been this way your whole life. What makes you think you will ever change? You will always disappoint people Monique. I knew these were all lies and it didn't surprise me it was being thrown in my face at the end writings of this book. With that being said, I was still emotionally worn out when I went to bed that night.

JUST BE STILL

I woke up having to make a phone call to cancel a weekend engagement I had previously planned. The person I called just so happened to lead a small group at our church about FREEDOM, which is her passion. She is so wise. While on the phone I told her my current struggles and how I have so desperately been trying to find freedom from these issues. I was running my mouth ninety to nothing and then she said it. "Monique, stop talking, you've GOT to stop talking." I quickly shut my mouth and listened. Her next words rang in my ears. "Monique, you've got to be still and let God handle it." Why is it hard for us to be still? Why is our first response to work at fixing something? Why do we run to our friends before we run to God? Why is it hard to let go and let God take over? I believe the answer is simple.

We are made up of body (flesh), soul, and spirit. Our flesh wants to call the shots pretty much all the time. It seems natural to work to fix something. We can see our flesh, we can see our efforts, and we can see our friends. It makes sense to start there. It's so much deeper. When we surrender to God, hand something over to Him, and become STILL, we truly find rest for our souls. Our minds find rest. Our emotions find rest. Our feelings find rest. We are telling God we trust Him when we hand something fully over to Him.

I know what you are thinking. My husband said the same thing to me when I was discussing this topic with him. You STILL have to work. You STILL have to find resolutions. You STILL have to DO something. Yes, yes, so very true. Being still doesn't mean you don't put forth effort. You are telling the Lord you trust Him. You believe He will open doors, create opportunities, and give you wisdom and discernment. All of those things will require action once they are presented to you. Let me tell you a story about hunting for sand dollars. It will hopefully give you a good visual example of the message I'm trying to portray.

THE SEARCH

My youngest daughter Alayna and I were on a mission to find sand dollars while at the beach. We are the exact same personality. If we are on a mission, we dive in and give 110%. The night before our epic expedition, we researched the best ways to find sand dollars. We read articles. We watched videos. We looked statistically where the best locations were, and times of day we needed to be there. Sand dollars were on my mind so much that I had a dream about a massive sand dollar that night. We woke up bright and early to beat all the others to the beach. We worked all morning. It's hard work finding sand dollars. The ones we were finding were tiny. Many would crumble in our hands when we touched them. The waves were crashing and pushing them away before we could snatch them up. We were getting soaking wet and hit by the waves as we worked. We walked away with our mission accomplished. We found 12 small sand dollars.

THE GIFT

Throughout the day sand dollars stayed on my mind. As I was drifting off to sleep, sand dollars were rolling in the waves as I tried to catch them. I know, I'm obsessed, sorry. The next day came along, and I was continuing to write on being still. I was still thinking about my insecurities. It was the day my friend told me to be quiet and be still. It was the day I was meditating on the verses about finding rest. It was the day I found peace. Right in the middle of all that, the Lord was about to drop the biggest visual example of this process to me. I am a visual person, so the Lord knew just what He was doing to make it crystal clear. I'm sure He thought this girl needs all the help she can get. I am so thankful He has so much patience with me. I probably wear Him out.

I walked back out to the beach to grab my chair I left out earlier in the day. On my walk out I was on the phone with Eric who manages our business and giving him a recap of how the day had gone. We were discussing some printing issues we were running into with this book. We had to change the plan we had been working on for over two months. Typically that would have stressed me out, but for some reason, I was at perfect peace. I was resting in the fact that I knew God had something better in mind. Our conversation then turned to the struggles I had been facing of feeling inadequate, and how quickly I found a sense of peace by being still. Somewhere during our conversation, I stopped in the middle of the soft sand and was standing still as we discussed BEING STILL. I looked down at my feet as we talked and I couldn't believe what my eyes were seeing. Was that a sand dollar? It was so tiny. It blended in with the white sand so you could hardly see it. It was perfectly intact, not a chip on it. I reached down and picked it up and carried on my conversation.

I finished my conversation with Eric and continued my walk back up to our house. I walked in silence, thinking how odd it was I found a sand dollar right there in the middle of the soft white sand. That was so random. How did it get up there that far from the water's edge? How did it remain intact being that tiny? How did I just so happen to stop right in the exact place where it would be at my feet? This was mind blowing after I had worked so hard the day before. That is when the Lord softly spoke to me, "You were still." I sat and thought about those words for a second. It was so true. Right there on the beach, I STOPPED in one place. I was standing still, finishing up my conversation with Eric about BEING STILL and finding rest. I looked down and effortlessly found a sand dollar, which wasn't so easy to find the day before. The epic expedition we set out on to find sand dollars was a serious mission. We fine tuned our skills by watching videos and reading articles. We got up early in the day to beat all the others to the beach. It was hard work. Sand dollars crumbled right in our hands as we went to pick them up. Waves washed many out of reach, and they were lost right before our very eyes. Oh, we did find sand dollars on our expedition that day, but this little treasure was something special.

This tiny sand dollar gave me a visual representation of what I had just walked through. When we quit working and striving in our own might, we find what we've been searching for. We find it when we are still and trust God. Did you catch that? It's not by working; it's by being still. It's easy to be still when you trust. Working will wear you out, don't you agree? We can research, read articles, and watch videos. We can see how others work through the same situations and replicate what they do. We can get up early before anyone else and work hard to find answers. We can think about it constantly. We can team up with someone and not take the expedition alone. Some of our efforts may crumble the second we try them. A few may seem right in our reach only to get washed away by an incoming wave of life that crashes and pushes it out of sight. We may find several that work, but they aren't quite perfect, not completely intact. It may get a little messy in the process when life hits and knocks our feet out from under us. We WILL see the fruit of our hard work, but it will probably leave us exhausted. Could there be a way that was easier, effortless maybe? Could we stop for one second, be still, look down and find the answer we were looking for when we weren't even looking?

I added that tiny sand dollar to our collection. The others were special, but this one was extra special. This sand dollar taught me a lesson. It was a symbol of rest. It was a symbol of handing something over to God and allowing Him to bring the answer in His timing and His ways. That's how the Lord works though, right? He drops things right in front of us when we stop striving and start surrendering. It may be in the form of something tiny when we aren't even looking, and the best part, it was effortless. Thank you, Jesus, for your ways. I will leave you with two verses to memorize and think on. Let's pray.

> Be still and know that I am God...
>
> *Psalm 46:10 (NIV)*

> But they that wait upon the Lord shall renew their strength; they shall mount up with wings as eagles; they shall run, and not be weary; and they shall walk, and not faint.
>
> *Isaiah 40:31 (KJV)*

Jesus, you never cease to amaze me. I thank you for speaking to us in the most unimaginable ways. So many times we strive in our might to find answers and resolutions to things we face in life. We feel worn out and defeated. We surrender to you and rest in your timing and your ways. We have faith and know you will take care of our needs. I pray for those who are reading this today that feel hopeless and defeated. Lord, bring rest to their souls. I pray you bring rest to their minds. I pray you bring rest to their emotions and feelings. As my friends begin to hand things over to you, may they be still and know that you are God. I thank you again, Jesus, for all you are doing as we draw close and seek after you. We love you and thank you for all your many blessings in life. We are grateful for the lessons we learn during the hard times we face. Your ways are perfect. Amen.

WALK IT OUT

1 Don't neglect a day of rest. Take time to refuel and reflect.

2 Blast worship music when stress consumes you. Lift Jesus higher with your praises, and in the process, He will become bigger than your problems. Hey, don't just wait for times when you are overwhelmed. Listen to worship music every single day. Worship at home, driving in traffic, or as you are drifting off to sleep.

3 Feeling exhausted and defeated? When these emotions wash over you, stop and hand control over to God. Pray for wisdom and discernment. Find rest in trusting in His promises. When doors open, walk through them.

4 Memorize and meditate on Psalm 46:10 and Isaiah 40:31.

NOTES

....
....
....
....
....
....
....
....
....

NOTES

DAY 17

NOTES

DAY *Eighteen*
COMPETITION
COMPLEMENTS
YOU

Hello, hello! After a day of rest, we are going to transition into a topic that could be a little stressful. Hang in there with me. I'm so glad you are trucking right through all these days. You are a rock star. I'm sure you are sticking with this better than anyone else. Your friends who are doing this same study have nothing on you. Yep. You are putting way more thought into it. Oh, wait. There were a few people who memorized the verses quicker than you did. I forgot about that point. Now that I think about it, they also spent several hours throughout the day pondering the questions that were asked in each day's topic. I honestly don't think it's fair they decided to do the same study you were doing. The nerve. Didn't they see you bought your book first? I heard a few did two or three topics a day to get ahead of you. They are cheaters. I knew it. They need to go back and read the day on integrity. Shady. You should report them. If you are friends with them on social media, you need to un-friend them immediately. You also should do a post explaining how evil and bad they are, that will prove you are the better person. If I were you, I would work harder the last three days to crush them. You can get ahead of them if you try hard. You need to win. You must win. GAME ON!

WE'RE ON THE SAME TEAM

The above situation sounds silly, right? Of course it does. However, we think like this each and every day in regards to those we believe are our competitors. In the scenario above, the other person doing the study wasn't a competitor. They simply were on a mission to grow in life and devote time to prayer, just like you. They are on a journey. You are on a journey. They are seeking after freedom. You are seeking after freedom. They would like to discover their unique design. You would like to discover your unique design. They have hurts. You have hurts. A competitor isn't a competitor unless you have decided there's a competition. This statement goes for the silly story above and in your business. Let me show you how.

Let's check out the definition of a competitor.

- *Someone who is trying to win or do better than all others especially in business or sports: someone who is competing.*

DAY 18

I'm not sure what your line of business is in life, but I am confident you have what the world sees as a direct competitor. You may have another business or person who wants to win or do better. They are trying to find more success. Maybe they want to crush you. Could it be possible they want to see you fail? I wouldn't put it past some to compromise their integrity so they can get one step ahead of you. With all that being said, you can't control how someone else thinks or acts in life. You can, however, control how you think and act. Competition can make you better or bitter. Competition can complement you or control you. Competition can bring out the best in people or the worst in people. Be the person who takes the high road. In a world of cut-throat business, you will stand out and shine. Before we move on, list out a few people or companies you feel are your competition, whether it's in your eyes or the world's eyes.

....

....

....

....

....

DAY 18

Apparently, competitors have been around since the beginning of time. Check out what Paul says in Galatians regarding competition.

> Pay careful attention to your own work, for then you will get the satisfaction of a job well done, and you won't need to compare yourself to anyone else. For we are each responsible for our own conduct.
>
> *Galatians 6:4-5 (NLT)*

That pretty much sums it up, right? The end. We can close up shop and move right to day 19. Wait, let's not do that, I would like to examine this verse a bit more. There are many useful nuggets in these two verses. First, I love that he said to pay CAREFUL attention to your work. Examine very carefully what you do, why you do it, and what the heart is behind it? He also used the word OWN work. He didn't tell us to examine the work of others but to pay careful attention to our OWN work. What happens when we begin comparing our work to others? We either think we are better than they are, or they are better than us. Each will be equally damaging. One slows you down because you think you will never measure up. The other slows you down because you think you have it all together. You have no need to improve. You are at the top. This is not good.

Compare yourself to yourself. If you have to start poking around in someone's business, let it be your business. Can you think of times when you compared yourself to others? Did it slow you down? Explain.

....

....

....

....

....

....

A LOOK IN THE MIRROR

The verse goes on to say that when you pay careful attention to your own work, THEN you will have the satisfaction of a job well done. The satisfaction doesn't come from paying careful attention to how you crushed the competition. The satisfaction doesn't come from being better than someone else. The satisfaction comes because you were focusing on you and your mission. The deep fulfillment comes from embracing who you were designed to be. When you discover this secret in life, you no longer have to compare yourself to others. When others succeed, it doesn't mean you failed. You don't measure yourself to others. You measure yourself to yourself.

Finally, the verse ends with saying we are each responsible for our own conduct. I would like to show you two other translations of this verse to open our eyes a bit more.

> For every man shall bear his own burden.
>
> *Galatians 6:5 (KJV)*

> ...for each one should carry their own load.
>
> *Galatians 6:5 (NIV)*

In the three translations, we find the words, conduct, burden, and load. The actual Greek word used here is "phortion." According to the Strong's

Concordance, it means a burden which must be carried by the individual. As something personal and hence is not transferable. It can't be shifted to someone else. The root word for phortion is phortos, which is load or cargo. When I hear the word load or cargo, I immediately think of HEAVY. Our own load is heavy, but when we throw on the cargo of someone else's actions, it's just too much to withstand. I don't know about you, but I have enough things I need to pay careful attention to. I have plenty of stuff I need to work on and improve in my life. If other people are playing dirty and out to crush you, let that be their burden. You are paying attention to your cargo. If other people are lacking in integrity to get two steps ahead of you, let that be their load and not your load. You have enough on your plate, and if you pick up all their cargo, that plate will shatter. How does it make you feel when you begin worrying about the dealings of others?

DAY 18

....

....

....

....

....

....

....

....

....

Now before we touch on this last point, I must make a confession. I am a VERY driven individual. With that drive comes a LOVE for a good competition. When we have family game night at our house, someone ends up crying. Please don't send me hate mail. I will never forget the time Alyssa, our oldest daughter participated in a wooden frog jumping contest on a cruise we went on. Oh boy, Jeremiah and I were cheering on as if she were about to win a gold medal at the Olympics. Seriously, it was probably embarrassing. If you were there that day, I'm sorry. Now hear me out. There is nothing wrong with being driven. Jeremiah and I may have gone a little overboard that day in the middle of the wide open sea, but let's not focus on our downfalls. We will both read through this day's topic three or four extra times. The point I would like to close on is this; we can allow competition to consume us or complement us. Let's discuss this for a bit and then close in prayer.

Competition complements us when we focus on bettering ourselves. Competition consumes us when we focus on being better than someone else. Real satisfaction comes from what complements you.

Remember the definition of a competitor?

- *Someone who is trying to win or do better than all others especially in business or sports: someone who is competing.*

The only person we need to be doing better than is ourselves. We need to be our only competitor. When you began this journey of *21 days of prayer for your business*, you were focusing on you and your business. You were not focusing on the businesses of others. You wanted to lay a foundation by giving God control of your life and business. You are moving in the right direction. Don't get sidetracked by picking up someone else's cargo. Tote your own load. I'm sure it's heavy enough. I want to leave you with some good news. Check this out, and then let's pray.

Then Jesus said, "Come to me, all of you who are weary and carry heavy burdens, and I will give you rest. Take my yoke upon you. Let me teach you, because I am humble and gentle at heart, and you will find rest for your souls. For my yoke is easy to bear, and the burden I give you is light."

Matthew 11:28-30 (NLT)

Jesus, you told us to come to you if we were weary and if we carried a heavy load and you would give us rest. We realize our own loads are often overwhelming enough. We bring those to you. We ask for you to teach us because we know you are humble and gentle at heart. We thank you for the rest you bring to our souls when we come to you. We thank you that your load is light. Open our eyes to the times we pick up the cargo of others. We don't compare our success to others, and we don't compare our shortcomings to others. Forgive us for the times we take joy in the struggles we see others face. Forgive us for allowing those struggles to make us feel better about ourselves. Our value and fulfillment come from you. We thank you for the opportunities you have brought our way and the doors you have opened. Lord, we honor what you have put before us by focusing on those blessings rather than what you have blessed someone

DAY 18

By permission. From Merriam-Webster's Collegiate® Dictionary, 11th Edition ©2016 by MerriamWebster, Inc.

else with on this journey. This journey of life is about so much more than the material things we acquire and trophies we may receive; it's about eternity. How quickly we get caught up in earthly things. Forgive us. We love you Jesus with everything that is inside of us. Be with my friends as they go about their day. Amen.

WALK IT OUT

1 Look at your list of those you view as possible competitors. Think of all their positive qualities. Concentrate on the good things they possess and not the negatives. Write these out in the notes section. How can you allow this to make you better rather than make you feel inferior or insecure?

2 Fight the urge to speak negatively about those you may see as competitors. Take the high road at all times. Never tear down others to build yourself up. Go out of the way to speak life and show love at all times.

3 Become more aware of the emotions and feelings you experience when you carry the load of others. When these times come, STOP, and hand them over to God.

4 Memorize and meditate on Galatians 6:4-5 and Matthew 11:28-30.

DAY 18

NOTES

DAY *Nineteen*

EXAMINE YOUR EXPERIENCES

You have made it to day nineteen. It's the home stretch, and there is no giving up now. How do you feel? Are you feeling refreshed and energized? Have you seen growth in specific areas of your life? Oh, I hope so. I have another question for you. On this journey, do you feel you've taken one step forward and two steps back when dealing with certain topics? I felt that way a few times, while writing this book. It's pretty ironic, but I didn't see those times as a setback, rather progress. How could that be? Realistically, if you took one step forward and then two back, you are BEHIND where you started. Many would think that, but you and I think differently. We take those experiences and examine them to make us better. When we are done examining, we are MANY steps ahead of where we started. Today's topic is about just that, examining our experiences.

EVALUATED EXPERIENCE

John Maxwell is an amazing author and speaker on the subject of leadership. One statement I have heard him say many times is that experience is not your best teacher; evaluated experience is your best teacher. I couldn't agree more, and it's something I practice in my life daily. We have made this a key component in our business. As a team, we examine almost every single thing we do. We examine the significant experiences as well as the experiences that may seem smaller. If we host a large event, we will examine the experience. When we finish up a business meeting with a possible supplier, we will examine the experience. If a hard phone call is made to someone that is upset, we examine the experience. No experience should go unexamined. So how do you examine your experiences? What questions do you ask? I'm so glad you are eager to know. Let's dive deep into today's topic.

When examining your experiences, ask yourself the following questions.

- What were the results? Was it a positive experience or a negative experience?

- Why was it a positive experience or a negative experience? What factors played a key role in it being positive or negative?

- How can I continue to embrace those positive results in the future?

- What can I learn from the negative results that were experienced? What can I do better the next go around?

- How did I feel overall about the experience? Was it hard? Something I enjoyed? Did it involve my skill set? Did it line up with my passions?

The list could go on and on. Bottom line, you need to LEARN from the experience. You LEARN by examining. Ask the Lord to open your eyes, to give you wisdom and discernment as you examine the things you walk through. You will experience so much growth from the process of self-examination. Don't allow these times of evaluation to get you down or make you feel condemned. You will often see things you need to improve or work on, but that doesn't mean you are a loser in life. You may have taken one step forward and two steps back, but through the process of examining that experience, you GROW! We talked about growing earlier in our time together. Growth can be painful, but I believe you are going to push through that pain and be a better person on the other side. Why don't I air my dirty laundry again to give you hope?

BUSINESS MEETING FREAK OUT

We recently had a meeting with a possible new supplier that turned out interesting. The nicest young man greeted us as we arrived and gave us a tour of their facilities. He gave a glimpse into his life by telling us he had just recently gotten married and this was a new position for him. His father was the owner of the company, and he was excited to be learning the ropes and following in his footsteps. When the tour was over, we sat down to talk business. I'm just thinking how sweet this guy is and how awesome that he's carrying on the family tradition. I'm looking at all the pictures sitting on his desk and hanging on the walls, and then I hear Eric Hudson, our business manager, say something I wasn't prepared to hear. Let me give you some details first.

We worked on one small project with this company in the past, and the quality they produced was not up to our standards. Eric decided we needed to address this right when the meeting began. It took me by surprise. Any rational person would understand this is just business, makes sense to address. For the individual who dislikes awkward moments such as these, it can be a terrifying experience. Eric, like always, addressed the issue with grace. He did say the quality they produced on our last project was not excellent. When I heard those words, I went into an instant panic and "fix the situation" mode. This sweet, young, recently married, wanting to take over the family business guy is probably feeling horrible. Does he know what to say? Was that a punch in his gut? Does he feel like a failure? My mind went into overdrive and so did my mouth. I profusely began to take responsibility for the poor quality.

It had to be our fault. We were working on a tight timeframe. I should have known a dark gray cover could have print quality issues. I was sure they were making the books so fast for us, that they were packing before the ink had dried. This could have caused the smearing of the ink. I went on and on for no telling how long. We finished up the meeting and left.

Once we got in the car, Eric looks back at me and asks, "What in the world happened in there? What was that all about?" I'm not sure what he is talking about until he brings up my freak out experience. OH, THAT. Well, you see, I felt so sorry for the guy. He was so sweet. He just got married. He gave us such an excellent tour. Eric jumped in and helped me see it differently. None of that had to do with the quality of the product we received or wanted to receive in the future. Telling this young man the quality was poor, was not telling him he was a horrible person. On the contrary, the honest feedback provided the young man with information he needed to improve his company. I learned a big lesson that day. I grew. The growth didn't come by me walking into that meeting, which was the experience. The growth came by me examining the meeting and my actions. Some would say I took one step forward by entering a meeting and two steps back by the way I acted in the meeting. That would be true had I not examined my actions, which left me two steps ahead of where I started.

YOUR TURN TO EXAMINE

Are you up for a challenge? I would love to reflect on all we have walked through together over the last eighteen days. We have had the "experience," but let's examine that experience. Pull out that pen, because you are going to have a little bit of writing to do. Think about the topics listed on the next few pages. Examine your experiences that came from your focused time of prayer and study. Was it easy for you? Did it pull up some deep hurts? What were the positives and negatives? How did you apply that topic to your life? How did you grow? In what ways were your eyes opened? How did God speak to you during your focused time? Once you are finished examining the days, we will close in prayer.

DAY 19

DAY 1 – GIVE GOD CONTROL

....
....
....
....
....

DAY 2 – FREEDOM FROM THE PAST

....
....
....
....
....

DAY 3 – YOU ARE UNIQUELY MADE

....
....
....
....
....

DAY 4 – CATCHING A VISION

....
....
....
....
....

DAY 19

DAY 5 – BE INTENTIONAL

DAY 6 – ALWAYS GROWING

DAY 7 – DON'T GIVE UP

DAY 19

DAY 8 – LIVING A LIFE OF WORSHIP

DAY 9 – EMBRACING EXCELLENCE

....
....
....
....
....

DAY 10 – PERFECTIONISM WEIGHS YOU DOWN

....
....
....
....
....

DAY 11 – CREATIVE PROBLEM SOLVING

....
....
....
....
....

DAY 19

DAY 12 – BUILD COMMUNITY

....
....
....
....
....

DAY 13 – SURVIVING CONFLICT

DAY 14 – FIGHT FOR YOUR FAMILY

DAY 15 – INTEGRITY MATTERS

DAY 19

DAY 16 – BE COURAGEOUS

DAY 17- BE STILL

....
....
....
....
....

DAY 18 - COMPETITION COMPLEMENTS YOU

....
....
....
....
....

Thank you for taking the time to think about each day's topic. You are growing more than you can ever imagine through this process. What you are doing is amazing. Allowing God to have His hand in the process is priceless. You are pressing on and not giving up. I love what Paul says in Philippians, check it out.

> Not that I have already obtained this or am already perfect, but I press on to make it my own, because Christ Jesus has made me his own. Brothers, I do not consider that I have made it my own. But one thing I do: forgetting what lies behind and straining forward to what lies ahead, I press on toward the goal for the prize of the upward call of God in Christ Jesus. Let those of us who are mature think this way, and if in anything you think otherwise, God will reveal that also to you.
>
> *Philippians 3:12-15 (ESV)*

Don't give up. Examine your experiences and keeping allowing God to be your foundation in all you do. Let's pray.

DAY 19

Jesus, we love you. Thank you for walking beside us each day during the past 19 days. We know that you are going to continue to walk beside us even after these 21 days are over. Every good and perfect gift comes from you. Our time with you is a gift. This gift is priceless. We thank you for that Jesus. Lord, I pray for my friends and all they have experienced during our time together with you. Help them examine each day's topic and how you can help them grow through the process. It's not an accident they devoted this time to you. I know you have a plan and a purpose for their lives and the things they learned while drawing close to you. Make that plan clear. Show them ways they can encourage others with what they have experienced. We will continue to press toward the goal to win the prize for which you have called us. We thank you again for all the many blessings you are lavishing on us. Be with my friends as they go through these last few days of focused time with you. Amen.

WALK IT OUT

1 Evaluate your day before you go to bed. Did your values make it into your day? Were there lessons you learned? Keep a journal by your bedside to write out thoughts that come to your mind about your day.

2 Find someone who will be honest and give you constructive criticism. Talk through evaluated experiences with others. Ask hard questions.

3 Don't be defensive when others show you things you could improve or work on in your life. Welcome this advice and be thankful it is growing you into a more mature individual.

4 Memorize and meditate on Philippians 3:12-15.

DAY 19

NOTES

DAY 19

NOTES

DAY *Twenty*
SUCCESS DOESN'T EQUAL CONTENTMENT

Why hello there. We have two more full days together, and we are going to make the most of it. Let's not be sad that our time is drawing to an end, deal? We are going to be content right where we are at on this journey. Speaking of being content, that is exactly what we are talking about today. Out of all our days together, I pray you grasp the first topic, giving God control, and this topic the most. They both go hand in hand. I pray you see that as we spend time together today. Before we get started, how would you define contentment in your own words?

....

....

....

Let's look at the actual definition of contentment.

• *the state of being happy and satisfied, the state of being content.*

Now let's define content.

• *a state of peaceful happiness, the state of satisfaction.*

How did that compare to your definition? That is how Merriam-Webster defined contentment. Let's see how Paul defined contentment in the Bible. He said he found the secret. Check it out.

I know what it is to be in need, and I know what is to have plenty. I have learned the secret of being content in any and every situation, whether well fed or hungry, whether living in plenty or in want. I can do all this through him who gives me strength.

Philippians 4:12-13 (NIV)

In 2008 Jeremiah and I were in the process of losing a LOT of material things in our life. It was a hard time. We were pretty much at rock bottom in the finance department. We could no longer pay for our house or our car. I remember when our bank account had less than a dollar in it, many times being in the negative. A business we had started from the ground up was sold to help keep us afloat.

DAY 20

Relationships from that business were strained and brought more pain than losing material things. Times were tough, the toughest we had walked through since we began our life together. We had the most amazing sense of peace though during this time. Please don't confuse that peace with me saying it was easy. We cried many tears. We were embarrassed. We both had moments when we had to remind each other where our hope was found. We knew the secret Paul talked about was where true contentment was found. It was the best worst year of our lives. It was our lowest, but it's where I have felt Jesus the closest. I wouldn't go back and change that year for any money in the world.

The need we were experiencing that year in no way compared to the need Paul walked through over his life journey. The things we were dealing with were a cakewalk compared to Paul. Nevertheless, they were our struggles, and we found contentment in the same person Paul found his contentment. We agreed with Paul. I can do all things through HIM who gives me strength. Not in my own might, but with Jesus by my side. Our pastor did a sermon series called Pursuit of Joy when we were walking through this hard time. It rocked our world. The series still lives on our church's website. I'll share it with you at the end of our time together today. I encourage you to watch it. It was life changing for my family. Before we move on, do you mind sharing some of your journey? I asked this previously in our time together, but do you mind thinking on it one more time? Have you experienced hard times? What is your, "I know what it's like to be in need" moments?

....

....

....

....

....

....

DAY 20

I feel like I need to keep thanking you over and over for putting your all into our time together. I pray these times of reflection turn into major blessings. I'm not sure what your "need" time was, and maybe it's something you are currently walking through now. This one thing I know, Jesus can bring contentment. He can bring the same strength to you as He did to Paul, as He did for my family, and as He has done for countless others. He will bring peace and satisfaction right in the middle of the storm.

It's interesting that Paul speaks of finding contentment in the good times too. Did you catch that statement? He has learned to be content in any and every situation. Content when well fed or hungry, when living in plenty or in want. Does that shock you? How can we not be content when things are going good? You mean when we get married to the love of our life we can have moments where we are not walking in satisfaction? When our paycheck quadruples we may still lack in the peace department? How about that bucket list vacation we have always wanted to go on, that will bring satisfaction, surely, right? The dream house with the huge backyard will have us walking with contentment in no time flat. The scholarship our child gets to the best college will fulfill us, correct? The new car will be the winner of peace. How about that new outfit? When we lose weight? Could it be the job promotion? Oh, what about when everyone loves us and accepts us? Now hear me out, none of these things are bad. They are all good, they just will never satisfy. The problem comes when we allow these good things to fill a need in our lives that only God is meant to fill.

Let's visit what contentment means one more time. When we are searching for contentment, we are searching for peace and satisfaction. We have agreed on that point, right? We have this void in our life, and we need to place something in that hole to make us feel whole. Once it is filled, we believe satisfaction and peace magically appear. Everyone has this void. What each person chooses to fill this void with looks different. I have tried filling that void with so many things over the course of my life. Jeremiah, my girls, friends, careers, vacations, money, material items, recognitions, perfectionism, or at least the PURSUIT OF IT, my success, and the success of others are just to name a few. What are some things you've tried filling the void in your own life with over the years?

....

....

....

....

....

I'm sure many of the things you listed above were good. I would go as far to say they have brought you much happiness in life. The question is, did they fully satisfy? I love my husband and girls more than anything in the world. We are a very close family and spend loads of time together, but I know my deep-rooted contentment doesn't come from my family. I know what it's like to be miserable in a career. I also know what it's like to be doing what you were made to do and

DAY 20

having the time of your life along the way. My deep-rooted peace is not found in that situation. In the last three years I have marked off more bucket list vacations than I ever thought I would be able to take, not one filled that deep void. I have hit the top level of my company and my paycheck doesn't even make sense to me. I promise you, with everything inside of me, that money and rank has not one time fulfilled me. Success will never fill the void Jesus was meant to fill.

I need you to stop and think about what I said above. Success will never fill a void that Jesus was meant to fill. The same contentment I have at the top level of a company; is the same contentment I had when I was the low man on the totem pole. You may not believe me, but I mean that from the bottom of my heart. Can I tell you a secret? There have been times at the top when I had to remind myself where my hope and peace were found. I believe this is a constant process of being content in every situation. All of this can only be done through Him who gives me strength. Let's read that verse one more time.

> I know what it is to be in need, and I know what is to have plenty. I have learned the secret of being content in any and every situation, whether well fed or hungry, whether living in plenty or in want. I can do all this through him who gives me strength.
>
> *Philippians 4:12-13 (NIV)*

If success is what you are aiming for, that is perfectly fine. I am all about you setting goals and believing in yourself. It's my prayer you figure out what you were made to do, catch a vision and go after it. I want you to find freedom and be intentional in all you do. I would love to see you stay on a path of growth. I want to see you find success. I want to see your financial worries wash away. I just don't want you to grab hold of those things and realize it wasn't what you were truly searching for in life. You will be left wanting more, I promise. I don't want you to find success and be surprised that it's not the magic formula of contentment. I am sure you can think of people who have found success in life, maybe all the money in the world, only to live out a life of misery and despair. Success is NOT a bad thing, it just will never fill a void only Jesus was made to satisfy.

How do you allow Jesus to fill that void? I thought you would never ask. You just accept the gift He has given us, His life. Jesus Christ came to this world to bring forgiveness to our sins. He paid the price so we didn't have to. He did that by dying on the cross. He did that for you and me. We don't have to earn our salvation. We just accept the gift He gave us. It's that simple. He wants your heart. He wants a relationship with you. You don't have to be perfect to come to Him. He doesn't want your perfection; He just wants you, flaws and all. I have been in church my whole life. It's only been in recent years where I truly have understood the difference between religion and relationship. It's not about a list of things to do and things not to do; it's about a relationship with the living God. When you discover that relationship, those lists become I GET to do those things, rather than I've GOT to do those things. Once you have encountered Jesus and the peace He brings, it's hard to be satisfied with anything else. The most rewarding and fulfilling thing I have done in my whole life is to embrace Jesus in every aspect of my life. It is my mission for people to know Him. It's my mission for you to know Him. All you have to do is tell Him you want Him to be part of your life. It's really that simple. You can tell Him that as we pray below.

Heavenly Father, we thank you for loving us so much that you sent your son Jesus to pay the ultimate price for our sins. He gave His life so we could live in eternity with you forever. He paid the price so we don't have to, thank you for that gift. We accept that gift you so freely gave us. Jesus, we want a relationship with you. We want you to walk along beside us. We give you control over every aspect of our lives. We understand that success will never fill the void in our lives that you were meant to fill. Forgive us for the times we allowed other things to take the place of you in our lives. We ask that you forgive our sins. We turn from our old ways and we want a new start with you. You make all things new. Thank you for that Jesus.

Jesus, today many reading this told you for the first time they wanted a new start. I can't even begin to put into words how thrilled I am they are going to walk out a relationship with you. I thank you for what was planted today. I thank you that what was planted will grow and not be snatched away by the worries or the pleasures of this world. What was planted WILL take root and grow and flourish. Their relationship with you will grow, flourish, and be prosperous. Again, we love you and thank you for who you are and all the many blessings you have lavished on our lives. Amen.

I want to share one last thing before we part ways. If you told the Lord today you wanted a new start and you wanted Him to be part of every aspect of your life, I would love for you to contact us at youinfuse.com/newstart. You need to know I'm jumping up and down doing the happy dance over here. The journey we are all on in life is about so much more than we really think. It's about others knowing and finding the hope of Jesus. I am so thankful you found Him. I love you more than you could even know.

DAY 20

WALK IT OUT

1 What are things that steal your peace and joy? What are things that make you happy? Will you write those out in the notes section provided for today's topic? This isn't a trick question. Enjoying earthly things isn't bad.

2 Develop a game plan to eliminate stressors in your life. Do financial struggles steal your peace? How can you work to kick debt to the curb? Are you miserable in your current career? Is it possible to change paths? How can you add more of what makes you happy to your daily life? Spend some time thinking and writing this out today.

3 How can you bless others? What are ways you can give back? Start where you are currently and apply these principles to your daily life.

4 Find some time to watch the following four messages from Church of the Highlands. It will rock your world!

- churchofthehighlands.com/media/message/no-matter-what
- churchofthehighlands.com/media/message/you-go-first
- churchofthehighlands.com/media/message/maintaining-your-joy
- churchofthehighlands.com/media/message/never-ending-joy

5 Memorize and meditate on Philippians 4:12-13.

DAY 20

NOTES

DAY *Twenty One*
GAME ON

Our last day together, can you believe it? I knew this day would eventually roll around. I have so many thoughts filling my mind I would like to share with you before our time officially draws to an end. First, I am thrilled you took this journey over the last 21 days. Oh to sit with you, even for just ten minutes and hear what amazing things the Lord did in your life. My mind can only imagine the wonderful stories I would hear. I also wonder if you had times of struggle. Did you feel like giving up? I'm thankful you are reading this because that means you pushed through. Were there times you felt the Lord was far away? Were there times you felt the Lord was so close? Did you find freedom from things that were holding you captive? I have a laundry list of questions for you, and I realize I may never hear those answers this side of heaven, and that's okay. I am confident the Lord began a good work in you and He will continue it to completion.

YOU WERE ALWAYS ON MY MIND

I want you to know how much you have been on my mind as I have been writing this book. I have been thinking about you and praying for you more than you could ever imagine. Countless others have been praying as well. Our prayer has been for you to have an experience with God. I pray you haven't just read words in a book, but you have actually had an encounter with God. As I was drifting off to sleep last night, I got to thinking about each day and what was written and I began to panic. We are getting ready for the final edit review and my mind wants to go into freak out mode. Did we catch every single grammatical error? Did the paragraphs flow from one to the next? Did each day even make sense? Was each day too long, not long enough? Did the titles for each day make a good fit? Did I ask the right questions? Did I share the right verses? Did I say anything that wasn't Biblically correct? Did I cover the right topics? Did I miss something important? I quickly stopped myself and told the Lord I trusted Him to use my words. I may not be a polished writer. I probably could have worded things differently here or there. A typo may be missed, but that's not what brings life change. Life change happens in the presence of Jesus. I didn't write this book to shout my name. I wrote this book to shout the name of Jesus. Somewhere in the middle of all my mess, I pray you encountered Him.

My mind now turns back to your thoughts. Did you realize during these 21 days how much our life issues affect our business dealings? When we are weighed down with insecurities, it's hard to lead others. When we are full of pride, there is less room for God to work through us. When fear overwhelms us, we can't move forward. When we don't know how we are designed, we can't be strategic with our gifts and talents. When lies are rolling around in our head, we can't walk in the truths before us. Conflict will cripple us. The list could go on and on. We can try to conquer those life issues by reading self-help books, attending workshops, or getting a life coach. None of those would be bad options. Jesus is the best one to turn to though. His ways are perfect. He will never leave us or forsake us. The Bible is packed with truths to help in each and every area of our lives. Ultimately, we can't do it on our own. Well, we could, but it's so much more fulfilling and effortless with Him by our side.

NO REALLY, HOW'D YOU DO IT

Speaking of needing Jesus; that brings me to yet another thought I must put out on the table before we part ways. I have come to the realization I will never be able to talk about success in business and not give God all of the credit. The business venture I pursued back in 2013 led to very quick success. I hit top levels in the company in record time. Immediately it caught the attention of executives, and they wanted to know what the secret was for this fast growth. Well if they wanted to know the secret, I had to tell them. Jesus. I explained how I devoted 21 days to prayer, found freedom, caught a vision, and embraced my unique design. That answer was good for about 10.2 seconds, and then an executive would pull me off to the side, and say, "no really, what's your secret?" I had that happen countless times. I would always laugh, lean forward like I was going to tell them something different, and repeat, Jesus. That was NOT the answer they wanted. I reassured them I did work hard, no question about it. I spent many hours understanding systems and processes. The Lord blessed me with a team of people who were rock stars when it came to business. If they wanted me to give them all those answers, I would. But I couldn't leave out Jesus. He is the foundation of my business, and I will always shout His name.

When I use the term "SHOUT HIS NAME," does that freak you out a bit? Please don't let it. I'm not saying I go around waiting for someone to turn the corner and scream "JESUS" in their face and scare them. That would be slightly awkward. I simply mean I give Him credit. I tend to be a little passionate. A word like shout is the first thing that pops into my mind. Shouting His name or giving Him credit will not always be the most popular path to take on your business journey. Don't let that stand in your way. You are not swayed by this world. Your eyes are set on eternal things. People may think it's silly you want God to be the foundation of your business. That's not your issue. That's their issue. People rejected Jesus back in the day when He was standing right in front of them and performing miracles before their eyes. Why should we think people would act differently today? When you love someone so much, you can't help but talk about them and sing their praises. The same is true with Jesus. We love Him so very much; we can't help but tell others of His great works. Never be intimidated by what the world thinks. You will walk in confidence and boldness because of your strong foundation and close relationship with Him.

NOW WHAT

Where do we go from here? Well, we take one step in front of the other each day. We pray without ceasing. We continue to draw close to Him. We continue to seek after Him. We thank Him daily. We ask for forgiveness daily. We pray for wisdom and discernment in all we do. Will we mess up from time to time? You bet we will. Does God leave us high and dry when that happens? I'm sitting here shaking my head no. Will we let people down on this journey? Probably. Will people let us down? I'm sad to say, but yes. Will people give you a hard time for embracing God? A few will. The world may not always be for us, but God is for us. Let's see what the Bible says.

> If God is for us, who can ever be against us?

Romans 8:31 (NLT)

Never forget this is a journey, and the journey isn't perfect. It's a process of growth. We will always be learning and growing. It's a beautiful thing. I can't even begin to tell you how much I grew while writing this book. Each day the Lord opened my eyes to things I needed to deal with in my own life. I found freedom, answers, direction, clarity, peace, rest, hope, and direction. I pray this time was as precious for you as it was for me. I needed these 21 days in my life so badly. Much of this writing took place while sitting on a beach in Florida. I am still here as I finish up this last day. I can hear the waves crashing as I type and my soul is at rest. I look out over the water and I feel peace. I don't want to leave. I don't want our time together to come to an end, but it must. I will pack up my belongings and drive back home to continue my journey. You will close this book and continue your journey. We both have good news though. The peace we experienced during this time together wasn't due to words on pages or waves crashing before us; it was found in Jesus. Our surroundings will change throughout our journey, but our peace in Jesus can remain constant. Even in the storms of life, He will be by our side and give us the same peace.

YOU = AWESOME

Before we part ways, I want to remind you of who you are one more time. You my friend, are a WORLD CHANGER. There is not one single doubt in my mind. You were made for great things; I know it. You have something to offer others. It doesn't matter what your past looks like, how educated you are, or what others have said about you. YOU ARE A WORLD CHANGER. You are not an accident. You are fearfully and wonderfully made for such a time as this. You were made to thrive, not just exist. Now, go out there with boldness and be who you were made to be. The world is waiting. I love you. Let's pray.

Jesus, I can't even begin to put into words how special this time has been with you over these last 21 days. I pray it's been as precious to my friends as it has for me. I can't thank you enough for bringing us all together to draw closer to you for such a time as this in our lives. I thank you for continuing to do the work you started in all of our lives as we part ways from one another. Our time may have come to an end together, but we always have you by our side. You stick closer than a brother. You never leave us or forsake us. Thank you for opening our eyes to things we needed to work on in our lives. Thank you for giving us wisdom and discernment. Thank you for the doors you have opened and the doors you will continue to open. Thank you for the confidence and boldness we will have to embrace each opportunity you put before us. Jesus we want others to know you the way we know you. We realize this journey we are on is about so much more than success in business. It's about eternity. It's about pointing people to your hope and your love. May we never forget that Jesus. I pray for my friends who started this journey and may have never had a relationship with you. Lord, show them how simple it is to surrender to you. You paid the ultimate sacrifice for our salvation. Jesus, you died for our sins. The love you have for us is unimaginable. We accept that gift you so freely gave to us. We know that it's just that, a gift. We can't earn it. We can't work for it. We just have to accept it, and we do. Thank you for this relationship we have with you. Lord, I thank you one more time for my friends who took this journey the last 21 days. I know you are going to do exceedingly and abundantly more than we could ever ask or think. Your ways are so much bigger than our ways and I can't wait to see what unfolds as we journey on with you by our side. We love you Jesus. Amen.

I would love for you to end with one final reflection of your time with God over these last 21 days. It could be a prayer for moving forward. It could be thanksgiving for the things He did in your life. It can be whatever you want it to be. I love you more than you could ever imagine and I hope you know you will continue to be in my prayers. GAME ON!

....

....

....

....

....

....

....

....

....

WALK IT OUT

1 How has the Lord worked in your life during these 21 days? Share with someone the lessons you have learned and SHOUT HIS NAME. Always give Him credit and point others to Him.

2 Don't stop drawing near to God. Continue to seek after Him and devote time to Him each and every day. Keep handing over control and asking for His wisdom and discernment in all you do.

3 NEVER GIVE UP. Remember, not to be a Debbie Downer, but the enemy is afraid for you to be who you were made to be. There is power in you walking out your unique design. You were made for such a time as this. The world will miss out if you throw in the towel. I believe in you.

4 Memorize and meditate on Romans 8:31.

DAY 21

NOTES

NOTES

WORDS THAT MAY NEED A LITTLE MORE EXPLAINING

Abundant Life (pg 40) – Life lived out in ALL CAPS and an EXCLAMATION POINT!

Armor of God (pg 15) – God's tools for spiritual battle found in Ephesians 6.

Captive Thoughts (pg 64) – Not allowing negative thoughts run wild in your mind.

Church of the Highlands (pg 37) – A crazy awesome church in Birmingham, AL.

Crazy Level (pg 15) - When something is kicked up to mind blowing level.

DISC Profile (pg 22) - Personality assessment that is WAY cool.

Fearfully Made (pg 18) – Made with great reverence or heartfelt interest.

Game Changer (pg 34) - Something that changes the course or thought process.

God Vision (pg 29) – A plan or direction God gives you.

Heavenly Father (pg 28) – God is our Heavenly Father. He offers only the best qualities of a father.

Iliotibial Band (pg 41) – A band that runs from your pelvis to your knee.

Life Giving (pg 65) – Focusing on the positive. Being uplifting and affirming.

MIA (pg 33) – Missing in action. You can't be found.

Number Our Days (pg 36) – Make the most of our time. Make each day count.

Paths Straight (pg 4) – Moving in a forward direction with ease.

Rest In You (pg 14) – Not stressing out because you know God will have your back.

Shut. It. Up. (pg 13) – Whatever was said prior to these words is mind blowing and needs to be read over and over.

Small Group (pg 89) – Small community of people who walk through life together.

Sparkle (pg 21) - You are shining because you are doing what you were made to do.

Spoke Life Over (pg 50) – Positive and affirming words someone speaks about you.

Such A Time As This (pg 21) – Being right now in the moment for a specific purpose.

Throat Punch (pg 13) – Totally ticked at someone and you want to inflict pain. Sigh, maybe we shouldn't condone violence. That's not very life giving. (haha)

Ugly Face Crying (pg 87) – Crying so hard you make a face only a mother could love.

Unique Design (pg 18) - Your specific design. (gifts, talents, personalities, and passions)

Words spoken over you (pg 10) – Positive or negative words people speak about you.

Works (pg 50) - Things you do in your own might.

World Changer (pg 50) - Using your life to impact others.

Worship Music (pg 56) – Music that is meant to praise and worship our God.

HEY *You!*

LETS STAY IN TOUCH!

@moniquemclean
@youinfuse

youinfuse.com

DIVE *Deeper*

INTO THE 21 DAYS OF PRAYER FOR YOUR BUSINESS!

CHECK OUT THE VIDEOS THAT GO WITH EACH DAY!

You can find them at
youinfuse.com